Gourmet Shops of New York

MARKETS, FOODS, RECIPES

SUSAN P. MEISEL & NATHALIE SANN

RIZZOLI
NEW YORK

FIRST PUBLISHED IN THE UNITED STATES OF AMERICA IN 2006
BY RIZZOLI INTERNATIONAL PUBLICATIONS, INC.
300 PARK AVENUE SOUTH
NEW YORK, NY 10010
WWW.RIZZOLIUSA.COM
© 2007 NATHALIE SANN AND SUSAN P. MEISEL

RECIPE, PAGE 164 [GÂTEAU DE CRÊPES]: © 2005, AMANDA HESSER,
FROM *THE NEW YORK TIMES*. REPRINTED BY PERMISSION. RECIPE,
PAGE 251 [SOPAPILLAS]: REPRINTED BY PERMISSION FROM *AUTHENTIC
HOME COOKING OF THE AMERICAN SOUTHWEST AND NORTHERN
MEXICO* BY CHERYL ALTERS AND BILL JAMISON (HARVARD
COMMON PRESS, 1995).

2007 2008 2009 2010 / 10 9 8 7 6 5 4 3 2 1

DISTRIBUTED IN THE U.S. TRADE BY RANDOM HOUSE, NEW YORK
PRINTED IN CHINA

DESIGNED BY: AISHA BURNES, ALSOKNOWNAS.INFO, NEW YORK

ISBN-10: 0-8478-2932-4
ISBN-13: 978-0-8478-2932-3
LIBRARY OF CONGRESS CONTROL NUMBER: 2006938976

ACKNOWLEDGMENTS

We would especially like to acknowledge Ted Sann, who stood by us during this amazing journey.

We are grateful to Charles Miers, as well as all the other people at Rizzoli who made the publication of this book possible, including our editor, Christopher Steighner, and Jonathan Jarrett. Aisha Burnes is responsible for the book's original design. And, of course, we are indebted to all the shop owners who welcomed us and shared their stories. Special thanks go also to John Brancati, owner of East End Books in East Hampton; Zeke Rosenson, from Spectra Photo; and Shawn Peterson.

Cooking is a collaborative act, and we depended on many gracious people who contributed recipes. Among them are Genevieve Deseglise, Ashyia Dudhia, Randy Fertel, Phyliss Frenkel, Haja Kaplan, Yvonne Lurie, Isabelle Mane, Flora Perez, Kenny Strauss, May Trent, David Waltuck of Chanterelle restaurant, Gary and Nina Wexler, and Marco Moreira of Tocqueville restaurant.

To the great loves of my life—
Louis and Ari.

—SUSAN MEISEL

To my family—Ted, Alexandra, Lizzy,
and Lucien.

—NATHALIE SANN

INTRODUCTION

BY **NATHALIE SANN**

Gourmet Shops of New York started with Susan Meisel's photographs. A few years ago, I came across Susan's wonderful book, *Hamptons Pleasures,* at East End Books in East Hampton, New York. I took the book home so I could continue to savor the luminous photographs of houses, beachscapes, and gardens.

Later that same year I found myself standing on line at the remarkable Cavaniola cheese shop in Sag Harbor waiting behind a woman with a full head of vibrant black hair. It was a mid-August day, in high season, and the line was long, so we got to talking, as people do on long lines in small shops. As it turned out we were both there to get our hands on some of the fresh burrata cheese that Cavaniola flies in every week from Italy. We talked first about the great local cheeses made at the twelve-cow Mecox Farm in Bridgehampton. From there we moved on to the great cheeses of the world and then talked about the best places to find them locally, each trying to top the other with some knowledge of arcane cheese or obscure store we had just discovered. But Susan knew all the stores I mentioned, and I knew all those she cited. It was a fromage standoff. It became clear that this lady not only shared my passion for food, but she also really knew her subject well.

Then we introduced ourselves, and I was delighted to learn that this was the same woman whose photographs I so admired. She asked about

my background and I told her that I learned to cook at an early age, making dinners for my large extended family at our country house in France. Ever since, I've been crazy about cooking and even more about finding the food that goes into making a great meal. I am lucky enough to know some of the world's great chefs and have cooked in places as diverse as a three-star kitchen and the galley of a ninety-foot Swan crossing the Atlantic. I have hunted truffles in Drome de Provence, picked morels in the woods of Fontainebleau, and fished for striped bass off Montauk Point. These days I cook mostly at our Sagaponack farmhouse where dinners for six generally end up as dinners for thirty. And I forage in the many, varied food shops of New York.

Susan and I quickly became friends and we began having dinner at each other's homes frequently. The table talk at these dinners was of course about food: Where'd you find this roast or that salmon? How did you prepare the gratin? It was in the course of one of these dinners—the men were deep into a conversation about golf, or politics, or the politics of golf—that we came up with the concept for this book.

Why a book about the food stores of New York? Guidebooks to our city are falling over each other on the shelves. But many of the guidebooks we've seen confine themselves to the island of Manhattan. Also, most conventional guidebooks stop at the address, with maybe a few words about items sold and a couple of vague opinions. What we wanted to do was to convey a sense of the ambience—the look and feel of a place from the moment you pass under the sign to the good-bye of the proprietor. Of course, you'll find stores in this book that you already know from your own shopping forays. But

it's our hope to lead you off the beaten track, to hidden pleasures and surprising discoveries.

This is a very personal book and entirely unscientific. We didn't do focus groups or laboratory research (although my husband served as a willing lab rat). We visited each of the stores in this book— and about five hundred others in all five boroughs. Our choices are totally subjective. Very simply, if we liked a store, it's in the book.

Amazingly, we disagreed on one store only, and we've vowed to keep its name to ourselves. Our friendship has thrived even after six months crammed into Susan's two-seat Subaru truck buffeting along potholed city streets. Each morning at nine, Susan would pick me up; we'd consult our maps, and then set out to Park Slope or Jackson Heights or Staten Island. More often than not we got lost and arrived at our destination only after the second or third try. We would usually enter a store cold, with no previous introduction to the owner, and we'd keep talking until any initial skepticism melted away. Before long we'd be sharing recipes and tasting everything in the place. (We might have gained a few pounds in the process.)

Usually we finished by four in the afternoon, the back of Susan's truck packed with the delicacies we'd picked up that day, to be sampled that same evening at dinner. We tried foods from every store that we visited; it was curry one night and kugel the next. Researching this book was truly a great exploration for us both. Neither of us had any idea of how vast Brooklyn is, nor of the diversity and longevity of the ethnic roots in many of the neighborhoods we visited. We heard Arabic, Hindi, Russian, Ukrainian, Yiddish, Spanish, Portuguese, and Greek. And we had more than a few adventures along the way. We visited one Greek bakery where no one spoke English. Suddenly a well-dressed, middle-aged man appeared and offered to be our interpreter. He guided us through our interview, and we were able to learn a great deal about traditional Greek baking. We thought this gentleman had been kindly brought in by the owners of the store. Then he invited both of us to come with him to the Aegean island of Skorpios, and we learned our good samaritan was in fact the resident neighborhood gigolo. (We let that one pass.)

We met only one shopkeeper who gave us a hard time. As soon as we stepped into her store she announced that she did not like our faces and that we looked evil. Then she proceeded to shout at us in a language neither of us recognized. We slowly backed out of the place and quickly crossed it off our list.

But all in all the proprietors were incredibly helpful and open. At an Indian market in Jackson Heights I asked a woman about a recipe and she patiently spent more than an hour explaining each step in intricate detail. For us it was like a National Geographic expedition for food, a great safari into the city's kitchens and bakeries to learn how things we'd never thought about are made, like doughnuts and dim sum. And the kitchens and production spaces ran the gamut from ultra high-tech to extreme old-world. Many of the hundred-year-old businesses also had ovens and cookers of the same vintage—maintained spotlessly, mind you. Some people refused to have their pictures taken, while others asked us to wait until they could gather the whole family.

Susan and I make an unlikely team. Born and raised in New York, she has lived her entire life here. I was born and raised in Paris. But what we have in common is a passion for good food, a lively curiosity about New York City and its people, and mutual respect and affection for each other. What we discovered over the course of our metropolitan travels is that New York is, right now, the food capital of the world. France has great food stores, but they all sell French food. Italy also has great food stores, but their products are regional Italian. In New York, in every borough, we marveled at the international sweep of products and purveyors, the vast expanse of places like Acme Fish and Eli's Bakery, and the dedication of stalwarts like Staubitz and Mansoura. In every case we were impressed by the amount of work that goes into this incredibly difficult business. If you want to work sixteen hours a day, six days a week, then open a food store. We were surprised again and again how the artisan tradition continues to thrive, not just in the making of high-end delicacies like cheese and chocolate, but also in producing staples like bagels and bialys. We were warmed by the family histories of the Di Robertis, the Russes, and the DiPalos, who own food shops going back one hundred years or more, and we were energized by the shoestring adventures of the new food entrepreneurs.

We hope this will inspire you to set off on your own food quest, and that you have as much fun as we did on ours. One piece of advice: take the time to talk to all of the remarkable people who run the markets. They are the real food experts, and you can learn more in conversation with any one of them than you can from any book.

IN THE BEGINNING: HUNTS POINT MARKET

There are no commercial farms within the boundaries of New York City. But part of the Bronx is still a huge farm—a virtual farm for the entire metropolitan area. In any given twenty-four hours, Hunts Point Market, tucked into an industrial corner of the southeast Bronx, moves more fresh vegetables, meat, and dairy products than what is produced in the entire state of New York in a day. Back in the seventeenth century, the area known today as the Bronx began as the farm and settlement of a Swedish sea captain named Jonas Bronck. The Hunts Point Market brings the Bronx—that vast sprawl of apartment buildings, expressways, stadiums, campuses, and factories— back to its roots. Five days a week, around the clock, twelve-wheelers come rolling through the gates, carrying goods from fifty states and fifty-five countries, off-loaded from freight cars, tractor trailers, and cargo planes. In the early hours of the morning, smaller trucks arrive from Manhattan, Queens, Brooklyn, New Jersey, and Westchester County—from neighborhood stores, restaurants, and supermarkets—and later depart loaded with enough fresh produce to last their stores for a single day or a week. The market is like a city within a city whose only business is food. Covering sixty acres and comprising forty-seven different wholesale merchants, it's the world's largest wholesale food distribution center. Because security is high, Hunts Point is closed to most visitors. But we thought it was important to include a peek of it here since the market marks a symbolic beginning in our culinary odyssey, and in New York City's food chain. Every sort of fruit or vegetable to tempt the discerning palate of New Yorkers passes through this mammoth gourmet market. But what was even more inspiring to us was the dedication of the multitude of workers here—there are more than ten thousand of them!— who are responsible for keeping the city's belly full.

1

CHINATOWN

As Little Italy shrinks, Chinatown is expanding east, west, south, and north, growing with all the excitement of a new immigrant community. This is the biggest Chinatown in the United States, the streets teeming with vendors selling fruits, crabs, toys, and umbrellas while trucks roll by loaded with cargo—baskets of shellfish, whole butchered pigs, crate after crate of the freshest vegetables. Every inch of Chinatown's sidewalks and floorspace is occupied by commerce, and most of this commerce is food-related. Streets once exclusively Italian are now 100 percent Cantonese. But, as Lou Di Palo, the well-known Broome Street salumeria owner explains, the Chinese have nurtured the heart and soul of Little Italy with their passion, enthusiasm, and love of good food.

Food fuels the frantic energy of Chinatown. And its food stores represent just about every region of China. From the well-known cuisines like Szechuan and Hunan, full of fire and spice, to more obscure traditions like Jiangsu and Anhui, slow cooking from the mountain regions, and Hubei, with its almost Japanese emphasis on presentation, a visit to Chinatown is a lesson in food, geography, and culture.

1. MAY MAY GOURMET CHINESE BAKERY

This forty-two-year-old bakery, hidden on a narrow street, makes dim sum for many of the best Chinese restaurants in New York. The good news is that May May doesn't sell only to restaurants. Dim sum, the Chinese equivalent of tea sandwiches—dumplings, buns, and rice dishes—are made in a dizzying variety of flavors and shapes. At May May, five enormous tin steamers prepare the ingredients—marinated chicken, Chinese sausage, vegetables, shiitake mushrooms, sticky rice, pork, bean curd, shrimp, and lobster. The wraps are baked in a separate oven, and the dim sum are then assembled by hand. Mornings, locals bring their own bowls and enjoy fresh dim sum with coffee. You can buy dim sum fresh or frozen: shrimp or Shanghai-style wontons, steamed pork buns, vegetable spring rolls. May May also sells a special soy sauce for dipping. A couple of boxes of dim sum in the freezer make excellent hors d'oeuvres or a wonderful light meal. Just put the frozen dim sum in a bamboo steamer and they'll be ready to serve in ten minutes or less.

2. AJI ICHIBAN

It would be easy to dismiss Aji Ichiban—a Hong Kong chain with more than ninety snack shops worldwide—as an Asian version of 7-11. But take a closer look and you'll pick up the delightful differences, from the sign at the door that encourages tasting, to the beautiful displays and packaging (all with English translations), to the vast selection of Asian treats. One side of the store is dedicated to salty snacks like dried fish, wasabi peas, and melon seeds. On the sweet side there's peanut nougat, dried plums, cola bottle gummies, and more. Try the tasty ten-scented olives, mixed with an unusual blend of ten spices, or haikkaido dried squid chips; the black currant gummies are outstanding.

3. NEW BEEF KING

Jerky—thin strips of marinated dried meat—was a staple of the Wild West. If a cowboy wasn't chewing tobacco, he'd be masticating a hunk of beef jerky. The word *jerky* comes from Quechua, a Native American language, so it was a bit surprising to find a beef jerky shop in Chinatown. As it turns out, just about every carnivorous culture has its own form of jerky. At New Beef Jerky, Robert Yee makes a product that is more tender and a lot juicier than the stringy, salty, jaw-wrenching American variety. Yee learned his distinctive jerky-drying technique from a great-aunt in Hong Kong. Instead of conventional dehydration, Yee painstakingly bakes the jerky by moving it from one oven to another, set at increasingly higher temperatures. The result is superb. Yee also makes ostrich and pork jerky. In any form, his jerky is a tasty all-protein replacement for high-carb snacks.

4. CHINATOWN ICE CREAM FACTORY

The dragon on the huge silk flag flying above the Chinatown Ice Cream Factory says a lot about this store. The dragon isn't fierce and fiery; he's fat and friendly, ready to slurp the huge ice cream cone in his right claw. Fun, fattening, and delicious, that's the spirit of this Chinatown landmark. The Seid family started the Chinatown Ice Cream Factory almost thirty years ago, adding exotic Chinese flavors to an American favorite—green tea, black sesame, durian, red bean, and taro, to name just a few. Join the crowds that gather every day beneath the dragon flag. You'll probably leave with a cone in your hand and a dragon T-shirt on your back.

THE ORIGINAL CHINATOWN
ICE CREAM FACTORY

華埠雪糕行

6

CHINATOWN ICE CREAM FACTORY

華埠雪糕行

4

亞那深海大刺參
South America
Dried Sea Cucumbers
每磅$69.50/LB

香港
生昌老牌鮑片
每磅$99.80/LB
半磅$50.00/1/2LB

智利黃花肚公
Dried Fish Maws- Male
每磅$48.80/LB

金昌隆精選
香港特級生晒响螺干片
Dried Slice Conch
每磅$22.00/LB
1/2LB. $11.50

南美超級花膠
Super Fishmaw
每磅 $68.80/LB.

5

5. KAM MAN FOOD

In Chinatown, they call Dean & DeLuca the "Kam Man of Soho." This two-story Chinese supermarket and kitchenware store is a one-stop immersion course in Chinese cuisine. A first visit can be daunting, but it's worth taking the time to study everything and ask a lot of questions. As you step inside Kam Man, you'll see Chinese signs everywhere; some have English subtitles, which make it a bit easier to navigate the store. Then take the leap, and buy a few items that catch your eye. Much of the food here will be new to uninitiated Westerners. Barrels and trays of pungent dried fish, sea cucumber, and various dried fungi stand at the center of the store. You'll see row upon row of sauces—fifteen different soys, plus hoisin, oyster, five-spice, and twenty varieties of sesame oil. Try the soft drinks in their unique bottles, stoppered with glass marbles. You may prefer the taste of kamune lychee to PowerAde. At the back of the store, choose from a dozen varieties of fresh noodles and fifty-pound bags of basmati or sticky rice. Downstairs, Kam Man stocks the most complete selection of Chinese cookware in New York, including woks of all sizes, with and without handles, nonstick and preseasoned. Experiment with new cooking implements—the long, flat spoons and ladles used for stir-frying, lethal-looking cleavers and chopping blocks, steamers, and rice cookers. There's an herbologist who sells the herbs and spices used in Chinese medicine. Before you leave, you might as well join the line at the front of the store for your serving of freshly roasted duck or squid.

JADE CHICKEN
KAM MAN FOOD / SERVES 2

One of the best things about cooking a Chinese dish is shopping for and preparing the ingredients: All of them are available at Kam Man, or you can wander through the markets and pick up what catches your eye. Then there's the chopping, peeling, boning, and skinning. The cooking itself, if it's done right, is over in a flash, with remarkable results.

**2 whole chicken breasts, boned
and skinned**

1 head of broccoli, cut into florets

3 tablespoons light soy sauce

½ cup chicken broth

1 tablespoon sesame oil

2 scallions, finely chopped

¼ cup sweet sherry

**Salt and freshly ground black pepper
to taste**

1   Put the chicken breasts in a soup pot with 4 cups water and bring to a boil over high heat. Lower the heat and simmer, covered, for 20 minutes. Remove from the heat and let the chicken cool in the broth. When cool, cut the chicken into bite-size pieces.

2   Cook the broccoli in a pot of boiling water until tender but still crunchy, about 10 minutes. Drain and let cool.

3   Make the sauce by whisking all the remaining ingredients together in a bowl.

4   Arrange the chicken and broccoli on a platter and pour the sauce on top. Serve at room temperature.

5

5

PORGIES

2 00

PICKEREL
PIKE

4 80

(SELECTED)

6

6. WIN CHOY FOOD MARKET

From early morning to late evening, this Chinatown fish store is packed with customers, fishmongers, and deliverymen. Win Choy restocks two or three times daily, making this the freshest fish in Chinatown. There are fewer and fewer real fish stores in Manhattan, so Win Choy has become a regular stop for Chinese and non-Chinese shoppers alike. The selection is dazzling. If a species lives anywhere near water, there's a good chance you'll find it on display here: octopus, squid, salmon, trout, striped bass, sea bass, sole, flounder, and porgy, available whole or filleted. The selection of shellfish is impressive: oysters, sand snails, hornshells, hen and sand clams, mussels, razor clams, and the more conventional littleneck and cherrystone clams. You'll also find crayfish and lobster, shelled and unshelled, cooked and uncooked, live tiger prawns, yellow shrimp, white prawns, and, in season, soft-shell crabs. At first glance, the tiny store might seem intimidating, with its frenetic activity and iced buckets of shellfish covering the sidewalk. But the fishmongers speak English and will explain the well-arranged displays—crustaceans to the right, fish in the middle, mollusks on the left, and toads under the counter.

CHINESE-STYLE STIR-FRIED SHRIMP

WIN CHOY FOOD MARKET / SERVES 4

Stir-fried seafood is one of the joys of Chinatown dining. This authentic recipe, using ingredients available at Win Choy Food Market, is remarkably simple and quite convincingly authentic. Bring this dish to the table in a white take-out container, and your guests will think you just picked it up on Mott Street.

This is a perfect dish for a very busy chef. It shouldn't take more than 20 minutes to make. Serve with steamed rice.

1 (1-inch) piece fresh ginger, peeled and finely grated

2 cloves garlic, minced

2 tablespoons soy sauce

1 tablespoon canola oil

20 ounces uncooked shrimp, peeled and deveined

1 pound bok choy, halved lengthwise

2 ribs celery, diced

1 cup unsalted cashews

Juice of 2 lemons

1 In a small bowl, combine the ginger, garlic, and soy sauce.

2 Heat the oil in a wok or nonstick frying pan over high heat, add the shrimp, and cook, stirring constantly, for 2 minutes.

3 Add the bok choy and celery and cook for 2 to 3 minutes, stirring occasionally, until the bok choy turns green but still has some crunch.

4 Add the ginger mixture and cashews and cook for 1 more minute. Remove the pan from the heat and stir in the lemon juice. Serve with steamed rice.

7. NEW YORK SUPERMARKET EAST

Beneath the Manhattan Bridge, on the site of a former Yiddish theater that later became a Chinese theater, you can walk through a pair of glass doors, and feel like you've traveled to old Shanghai. New York Supermarket East is not a stop on any tourist trek through Chinatown. This is a local supermarket, and because the local population is 99 percent Chinese, you will see only Chinese products, labeled in Chinese, tended by staff who speak only Chinese. While the demand for chicken feet, ox penis, and shark fin may be minimal above Canal Street, at New York Supermarket East they restock these delicacies daily. You'll find a huge selection of shellfish, baked goods, noodles, and rice cakes. Try the brown sugar candy sold in chunks, delicious in coffee or for making caramel sauce. There's a very good selection of cooking wines, and three or four kinds of tapioca. New York Supermarket East is worth the trip for the visuals alone, but look carefully and you'll discover a few new foods and new ideas.

RICE PUDDING
WITH ASIAN PEAR

NEW YORK SUPERMARKET EAST / SERVES 3

This is not a specifically Chinese dish, but the secret to great rice pudding is, not surprisingly, the quality and variety of the rice, and New York Supermarket East has one of the best selections anywhere. Use a different kind of rice each time for a different taste and texture, but always use real vanilla beans.

2½ cups whole milk

1 vanilla bean

⅓ cup sticky rice

1 large egg

¼ cup dark brown sugar

2 teaspoons salted butter

⅓ cup Asian pear, cored and finely diced

1 Put the milk in a medium-size heavy-bottomed saucepan. Split the vanilla bean lengthwise and add it to the milk.

2 Bring the milk to a boil, then remove the vanilla bean and, with a spoon, scrape the seeds from the vanilla bean and add them to the milk.

3 Stir in the rice and simmer over low heat, covered, watching carefully and stirring frequently so the rice does not burn, until the rice is tender, about 20 minutes. If the rice is too dry, add more milk. Remove from the heat.

4 In a bowl, whisk together the egg and brown sugar, then stir in some of the rice mixture a tablespoon at a time so as not to curdle the egg.

5 Add the mixture back to the saucepan and cook over very low heat, stirring, until it thickens. Do not let the mixture come to a boil.

6 While the rice is cooking, warm the butter in a small pan, add the pear, and cook over low heat for 15 minutes. Fold the pear into the rice pudding. Serve at room temperature.

7

8. ASIA MARKET CORPORATION

If you've ever tried a recipe from a Southeast Asian cookbook and stopped short at the prospect of finding kaichi, taro, and lemongrass at your local grocery, this market will supply these ingredients and more. The Asia Market Corporation specializes in Thai, Indonesian, and Filipino products. It's a great place to expand your culinary horizons, so bring your cookbook and browse the aisles. Happily, the products are labeled in English. The selection of Asian fruits and vegetables is comprehensive, as is the selection of fresh and dried herbs and spices—watercress, cilantro, lemongrass, scallion, dried chile, turmeric, coriander, and caraway. So, the next time a recipe calls for fresh coconut milk you'll be able to reach into your freezer for the quart you found at Asia Market.

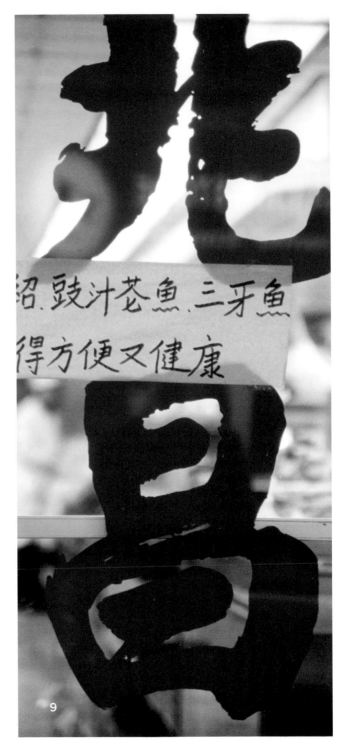

9

CHICKEN WONTONS

ASIA MARKET CORPORATION /

MAKES 2 DOZEN WONTONS

These are especially fun to make. Your guests might not believe you went to the trouble to make your own wontons, but once they bite into these fresh and tasty dumplings they'll be happy you did. You can get all the ingredients at Asian Market Corporation.

1 pound boneless, skinless chicken breasts

½ cup sliced scallions

½ cup drained canned water chestnuts, diced

1 tablespoon peanut oil, plus 1 cup if frying

1½ teaspoons salt

½ teaspoon freshly ground black pepper

1½ teaspoons cornstarch

2 teaspoons soy sauce

1 pound square fresh wonton wrappers

1 egg, beaten

1 bottle sweet-and-sour sauce from Asia Market Corporation

1 Chop the chicken breasts with a sharp knife into very small pieces. Mix the chicken well with the scallions, water chestnuts, 1 tablespoon of the oil, the salt, pepper, cornstarch, and soy sauce.

2 Take 1 teaspoon of the chicken mixture and place it in the center of a wonton wrapper. Brush three corners of the square wrapper with egg.

3 Fold the wrapper over, making a triangle, and press lightly to seal the edges.

4 To steam the wontons, place them in a bamboo steamer over boiling water for 5 minutes.

—or—

5 To fry the wontons, heat the 1 cup oil in a heavy-bottomed pot until very hot and, with a slotted spoon, carefully place a wonton in the oil. Add more wontons, but do not crowd the pot. As the edges turn brown, take the wontons out of the oil and drain on paper towels. Serve hot, with the sauce.

9. MULBERRY MEAT MARKET

At lunchtime, Mulberry Meat Market is invaded by an army of hungry workers who head for the steam tables of prepared food—extremely cheap and good. You may want to wander over to the giant counter for the fresh and marinated meat ready to be cooked at home. Try the flank steak or the marinated chicken in spicy sauce. The refrigerator at the back of the store displays chickens and Chinese sausages, as well as more exotic meats.

10. TEN REN TEA

Two walls of this narrow shop are covered floor to ceiling with beautiful tin canisters filled with different varieties of teas and herbs. You'll find green tea, jasmine tea, oolong, king's, which is oolong blended with ginseng and comes in green and dark varieties. There's the traditional black tea, and mountain grown white tea, which has a high concentration of purportedly beneficial polyphenols. There's Pou Chong, a fermented green tea, Pu Erh, and Ti Kuan Yin, an earthy postfermented Chinese tea. That list hardly cracks the surface: This is the place to learn everything about tea, and the people behind the counter are more than willing to explain their wares. The teas come loose or in bags, depending upon your preference. Ten Ren also carries a large selection of ginseng in tea bags, as a powder, and as raw roots in capsules. What ginseng actually does is open for debate, but what it's supposed to do keeps customers lined up nine deep at Ten Ren's ginseng counter.

11. ORCHARD SAUSAGES INC.

If you've never heard of Chinese sausage, one trip to Orchard Sausages will fill this gap and add new breadth to your cooking. This hard-to-find Chinatown business is more factory than store. Every square inch of the tiny shop is dedicated to sausage—on ropes, on racks, and in boxes, drying, dried, and ready to eat. Chinese sausage—made from pork and ample amounts of fat, then lightly smoked and sweetened—is smaller and thinner than Western sausage. Add them to soup or mix them with rice, paella-style.

12. KING WAH BAKERY

We found this traditional Chinese bakery by following the sweet scent of baking cookies. Aside from American fortune cookies, King Wah makes more authentic treats like Chinese cheesecake, shrimp chips, almond cake, chestnut bread, and black bean pie. They also make a delicious lotus seed cake for the Chinese New Year. There are a few seats in the back, so order yourself a hefty slice of lotus pie and a pot of oolong tea and settle in to watch Chinatown stream by.

9

10

11

12

10

13

13

13

13. THE FRUIT AND VEGETABLE STORES OF CHINATOWN

On a short stretch of East Broadway between Catherine Street and Allen Street, you'll find a series of extraordinary food stalls. Also on Bayard Street there's Hung Lee Co., where the fruits and vegetables are pampered, spritzed, and polished hourly. The displays are meticulously ordered, and every item is sold at its peak. You won't find a single wilted lettuce leaf in this store. At Hung Lee, you won't have to check the tomatoes for ripeness. Obsessive? Compulsive? Maybe, but the fruits and vegetables here are always perfect. Among the other outstanding spots for fruits and vegetables are Lou Cheng Market, New Lung Hing Market, and Number One Long Hing Market. Chinatown is a place to wander, explore, and discover, so use your nose, your eyes, and your cook's sixth sense and you're sure to find some great shops.

FRIED GREEN PLANTAINS

THE FRUIT AND VEGETABLE STORES OF CHINATOWN / SERVES 4

Although plantains are a Latin American ingredient, the green banana-like fruit has become a staple in China, India, and Thailand. We found these at Hung Lee. When the plantain is green it's very starchy, and should be fried or boiled. When the plantain is black it is at its sweetest and can be used uncooked for desserts.

2 green plantains

1 cup canola oil

Salt

1   Peel and slice the plantains into 1-inch rounds.

2   In a large frying pan, heat the oil. Place the plantain slices in the hot oil and fry for about 3 minutes, turning constantly. Remove the slices from the oil and place on paper towels to drain.

3   Place the plantains between two paper towels and carefully flatten each one with a wooden mallet.

4   Put the slices back in the hot oil for about 3 minutes and cook, turning, until brown.

5   Drain on paper towels and sprinkle with salt. Serve warm.

CHAPTER 2
EAST VILLAGE

The East Village, the area from Fourteenth Street to Houston, between Third Avenue and the East River, is the only part of the city where the avenues are designated by single letters: Avenues A, B, C, and D. In the 1970s and '80s the East Village was so tough locals said the D in Avenue D was short for "dead." But all that's changed, and for many of the old-line bohemians the area has been homogenized beyond recognition; for those of us who didn't experience the chaos of the early years the neighborhood retains a rough-edged charm.

In the late eighteenth century new waves of immigration turned the East Village, once home to New York's largest German community, into an outpost of Eastern Europe. This mélange of Polish, Ukrainian, Czech, and Russian immigrants was joined by a small cadre of Italians and Eastern European Jews. As each group arrived, they unpacked their traditional foods and recipes. Later, in the 1940s and '50s, the Eastern Europeans were joined by immigrants from Puerto Rico, the Dominican Republic, and Colombia, adding additional spice to the mix. In the 1960s there was a brief psychedelic flash—enter the hash brownie—as Jimi Hendrix, Jefferson Airplane, and the Grateful Dead lit up Fillmore East. Over the past twenty years, the neighborhood has been changing again as uptown types stream downtown into Alphabet City. Now old-school butchers, bakers, and pierogi makers stand side by side with new boutique bakers, ice-cream makers, and chocolatiers—traditional meeting trendy in a rich culinary landscape.

1. KUROWYCKY MEAT PRODUCTS

Everyone in the neighborhood calls this fifty-year-old pork shop "the place with the hams in the window." Kurowycky's produces everything they sell in-house, including the terrific ham, smoked in their own smokehouse, one of only two smokehouses in Manhattan. Kurowycky also makes kielbasa, kishka, krakiwska, mazurka, and kabanosy. The kishka is a Polish blood sausage made with buckwheat, pork, and spices. The krakiwska is ham sausage seasoned with garlic and pepper, and the kabanosy is a long, thin paprika-ed hunter's sausage served either soft or dried. Jerry, the proprietor, is the third generation of his family to work in Kurowycky. Jerry's a vegan, which seems next to impossible in this carnivore's fantasyland, though he never lets his diet interfere with his work.

NEW ORLEANS RED BEANS AND RICE

KUROWYCKY MEAT PRODUCTS /

SERVES 2 OR 3

This recipe was given to us by Randy Fertel, a transplanted New Orleanian who swears by Kurowycky's ham bones and kielbasa. A New Orleans favorite traditionally cooked on Mondays (washday) because the pot could be put on the stove and left to bubble into a rich and glorious natural gravy, the ham bone (here from Kurowycky) and its marrow giving the beans a creamy texture and smoky flavor. Kielbasa handmade by the same butcher adds more of the same smokiness. We prefer Camellia Brand beans, a New Orleans institution for over seventy-five years, available online. If you do not soak the beans, wash and add them to boiling rather than cold water. They will need to cook a little longer than soaked beans.

2 pounds dried red (kidney) beans, soaked overnight in cold water to cover

2 cups chopped onion

½ cup thinly sliced scallions

½ cup chopped green bell pepper

1⅓ tablespoons finely minced garlic

1 pound seasoning (baked) ham, cut into 1-inch cubes

1 large hambone with some meat on it, sawed (if possible) into 4- to 5-inch lengths

1 tablespoon salt, or less if ham is salty

½ teaspoon freshly ground black pepper

⅛ teaspoon ground cayenne

⅛ teaspoon hot red pepper flakes

2 whole bay leaves, broken into quarters

½ teaspoon dried thyme

⅛ teaspoon dried basil

1 pound kielbasa, cut into ½-inch slices

Boiled rice

1 Drain the soaked beans in a colander and put them, along with all the other ingredients except the kielbasa and rice, into a heavy 8- to 10-quart pot or kettle, adding just enough cold water to cover.

2 Bring to a boil over high heat. Skim the froth that may form on the top, then lower the heat and simmer for 2½ to 3 hours, until the beans are tender and a thick gravy has formed. During cooking, stir frequently and scrape down the sides and across the bottom of the pot with a wooden spoon or spatula to prevent scorching (a heavy pot and low heat will help).

3 One hour before the beans are done, add the kielbasa and continue to simmer. If the mixture appears too dry, add about 1 cup water toward the end of cooking. To increase the thickness of the gravy or if the mixture is too runny, remove and smash ½ cup of the beans and stir them back into the pot. When the beans are cooked, turn off the heat. To serve, ladle about 1½ cups of the beans, with meat and gravy, over a portion of rice.

3

HOMEMADE
- PIEROGIES
- STUFFED CABBAGE
- SALADS
- BLINTZES
- SOUPS.
- BEEF TRIPE
- HUNTER STEW /BIGOS

4

3

PANYA Bakery
10 STUYVESANT ST.,
NEW YORK .NY 10003

2

3

2. PANYA BAKERY

At 10 Stuyvesant, a street named after the last Dutch governor of Manhattan, you will find Panya Bakery, a slice of Old Japan. Panya turns out sweet and savory delicacies as elegant as those in the finest Tokyo bakeshops. Among the delightful sweets, ogura is a light pastry filled with red bean paste. The green tea tiramisù—Tokyo meets Tuscany—is terrific. The yuzu cake, made from a Japanese citrus, is tangy and outstanding. On the savory side, Panya makes marvelous curry takoyaki, subtly seasoned octopus dumplings, and, veering from the Japanese tradition, a delicious quiche of the week.

3. AUSTRALIAN HOMEMADE

St. Mark's Place is a tourist's carnival of T-shirt shops and tattoo parlors, but mixed with all the glitz are a few culinary high notes. One of the newest is Australian Homemade. Australians like their ice cream at near room temperature—almost melted—this, they believe, highlights the smooth, creamy texture and releases the rich flavors—chocolate chip, banana, strawberry cheesecake, crunchy macadamia. At Australian Homemade, you can watch them mix fresh batches of ice cream, so that while you're finishing off your first serving you can plan your second round. You can also sample from the handmade Belgian chocolates, each embossed with aborigine drawings, in sizes to fit an Australian appetite. Choose from an array of unusual and subtle flavors: Earl Grey with nut fragments, double chocolate with coffee and hazelnut, and creamy orange filling with coconut.

4. FIRST AVENUE PIEROGI & DELI CO.

The pierogi is the Ukrainian national dish, and this East Village store makes some of the best handmade pierogi around. First Avenue Pierogi looks like it was airlifted whole from a narrow street in Kiev. A handwritten menu displays the daily choices on a board outside the store. Making first-rate pierogi takes patience and skill. For the "skins," the bakers cut large, thin sheets of floury dough into four-inch circles. They then fill each skin by hand with a dollop of sauerkraut, potato, cabbage, cheese, meat, or some combination of these and then fold the filled skin into the traditional half-moon shape. The skins are pinched and sealed with the fingertips, giving the pierogi its distinctive serrated edge, and then boiled or steamed for ten to twelve minutes. First Avenue pierogi are remarkably light and full of flavor. Frozen, they will last for weeks, so even on short notice you can reach into the freezer and surprise your guests with these luscious dumplings, served with butter and caramelized onions.

5. EAST VILLAGE MEAT MARKET

East Village Meat is the other last smokehouse on Manhattan Island (after Kurowycky). Most of the customers speak Russian or Ukrainian, but, as the neighborhood changes, more and more non-Slav New Yorkers are discovering this shop. Five butchers serve up pork sausages and superb cuts of fresh pork: pork loin, pork roast, thinly filleted pork schnitzel. Loop upon loop of kielbasa, beer sausage, and garlic sausage are festooned on racks in the smoking room and in the temperature- and humidity-controlled drying room.

6. DE ROBERTIS

The blocks between Eleventh and Twelfth Streets off First Avenue are the epicenter of the East Village's small Italian enclave. One of the treasures is De Robertis pasticceria. Paolo De Robertis, a native of Puglia, opened his café over one hundred years ago, and the white tile floors, tin ceilings, dark wood chairs, and marble-topped tables make it easy to believe that it's still 1904. At the front of De Robertis, the original glass cases display biscotti, éclairs, amaretti, and cannoli. You'll also find cassata Siciliane, a ricotta-filled pastry covered with sugar icing and dried fruit; mille foglia, thin leaves of crisp crust filled with thick, creamy egg custard; sfogliatelle, a clam-shaped pastry filled with ricotta; and osso di morto, a sugar and flour biscuit. In the café's back room, the rich scent of dark roasted coffee blends with the sweet aroma of baking pastry. Patrons sip from tiny cups of intense black espresso, slurp cappuccino, and gobble down cannoli, while the third and fourth generations of De Robertis—there are eleven great-grandchildren—take the time to make everyone who comes through the door feel like family.

7. BLACK HOUND NEW YORK

Across Second Avenue from St. Mark's Church (circa 1799) is Black Hound (circa 1988), an upscale, relatively new addition to the East Village food scene. This tiny store exalts craftsmanship, from the wooden chest filled with wax-sealed jars of homemade preserves to the displays of chocolate truffles, cakes, and cookies, all made from scratch in Black Hound's own bakery. Their award-winning decorated cakes are not to be missed. The yellow-and-black bees swarming across the top of the Busy Bee Cake look real enough to buzz and fly away. This Shaker-inspired store is a joyful time-out from the rush and tumble of New York living.

7

7

6

8. RUSSO MOZZARELLA

Russo is a lot more than mozzarella. This tiny Italian grocery, almost hidden behind its hand-painted sign, is packed full of the finest Italian foods. Russo's pasta is made by hand—thick spaghetti, silky thin capellini, hearty manicotti, conchiglie, farfalle, and rotini. Russo's homemade sauces—amatriciana, puttanesca, and marinara—complement the aged Parmigiano-Reggiano and Romano cheeses, which can be hand grated or served in slices with Russo's olives, sausages, and salami. The bread, semolina and white, with and without sesame seeds, is crusty and fresh, ready for dipping into one of Russo's distinctive extra-virgin olive oils.

MOZZARELLA EN CAROZZA

RUSSO MOZZARELLA /
SERVES 4 AS AN APPETIZER

This simple appetizer depends entirely on the quality of the mozzarella. In Italy people shop for mozzarella every morning, and it's usually sold out before afternoon. In this recipe the subtle taste of Russo's fresh unsalted mozzarella is intensified by frying.

FOR THE MOZZARELLA EN CAROZZA

12 slices white bread, crusts removed

1 pound fresh mozzarella, thinly sliced

18 anchovy fillets, mashed to a paste

2 large egg yolks

1 (6-ounce) package panko (Japanese bread shavings; available at Japanese, Chinese, or Korean grocers)

1 quart vegetable oil for frying

FOR THE SAUCE

½ cup extra-virgin olive oil

12 anchovy fillets, mashed to a paste

½ cup (1 stick) unsalted butter, clarified

Freshly ground black pepper

MAKE THE MOZZARELLA EN CAROZZA

1 Cover 1 slice of the bread with cheese, then spread anchovy paste over the cheese.

2 Cover with a second piece of bread and repeat with another layer of cheese and anchovy paste, finishing with a third slice of bread on top. Repeat the same process with the remaining bread, cheese, and anchovy paste, to make 4 stacks (or "carriages").

3 Add 3 tablespoons water to the egg yolks and beat to combine.

4 Coat all 6 sides of the stack with the egg mixture, then coat with panko. Sprinkle additional panko over the top.

5 In a heavy pot, heat the oil until it reaches 350 degrees, then add the stacks one at a time and fry each until golden brown, turning once. Drain on paper towels.

MAKE THE SAUCE

1 Combine the oil, anchovies, butter, and pepper in a small saucepan. Heat through.

2 To serve, coat the bottom of each of 4 serving plates with sauce and place 1 "carriage" on top.

9. MOISHE'S HOME MADE BAKE SHOPPE

You will never see this ramshackle storefront in an architectural magazine; in fact, it would be easy to walk by Moishe's with a dismissive shrug. That would be a mistake, for Moishe's is a miracle of bread and pastry. Moishe is an ordained rabbi with piercing eyes and a billowing gray beard. He looks like a fierce Old Testament patriarch, but, as you'll quickly find out, he is all sweetness and light, with a joke for anyone who wanders into the bakeshop. Even the panhandlers off Second Avenue get a smile and a story. Moishe runs the store the old-fashioned way, writing receipts by hand, and tying string around the cake boxes. And Moishe makes world-class challah. He hand braids and glazes the honey-flavored egg bread then bakes it nut brown. Moishe's challahs are works of sculptural beauty, their braided crusts glistening in the low light of the shop. But challah isn't all they make at Moishe's. Try the crisp bow-tie pastry or the thin, board-shaped kichels stacked in the window like so many sheets of paper, the egg kichels made of the same buttery batter. Moishe makes hamantaschen for the Jewish holiday of Purim—the tricornered pastry symbolizes evil King Haman's hat and is filled with sugary prune, poppy seed, or apricot puree. The strudel, as flaky as any in Vienna or Budapest, overflows with tart apples and sweet raisins. And many claim that Moishe's has the best babka in New York, Greenpoint included.

CHALLAH PUDDING

MOISHE'S HOME MADE BAKE SHOPPE /
SERVES 4 TO 6

Moishe's delicious variation brings bread pudding to a new level. The recipe adds raisins and homemade caramel to Moishe's egg-and-honey challah. It makes a sweet and satisfying winter dessert.

1 cup raisins

⅓ cup rum

2 cups sugar

4 cups milk

1 vanilla bean

4 large eggs

3 pounds challah

1 Marinate the raisins in the rum and ½ cup water overnight. Drain.

2 Preheat the oven to 375 degrees.

3 In a saucepan, mix together 1 cup of the sugar with ⅓ cup water. Cook over high heat until the mixture turns a rich amber color, about 5 minutes.

4 Remove from the heat and pour the caramel into the bottom of a soufflé dish and turn the dish to coat the sides.

5 To the same saucepan, add the milk and vanilla bean. Heat the milk over medium heat; when it starts to simmer, remove from the heat and let it cool for 20 minutes.

6 Remove the vanilla bean and slice it open lengthwise with a knife; scrape the seeds into the milk.

7 With an electric mixer, combine the eggs and the remaining sugar, beating well, then gradually add the milk mixture, stirring constantly. Set aside.

8 Trim off as much of the challah's brown crust as you can. In a large bowl, tear the challah with your hands into large pieces.

9 Pour the egg mixture over the challah and mix well with a wooden spoon.

10 Pour into the soufflé dish and place it in a larger pan with 2 inches of water.

11 Bake for 45 minutes, until a knife inserted in the center comes out clean. Serve warm.

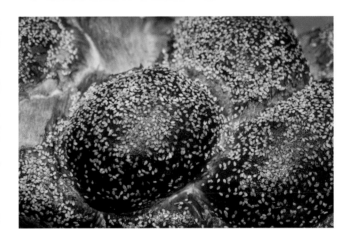

CHAPTER

3

FINANCIAL DISTRICT & TRIBECA

Until the late 1950s the area now called Tribeca—the triangle below Canal Street bounded by Broadway on the east and by the Hudson on the west—was almost totally dedicated to meat-and-potatoes commercial enterprise. Textile mills and flange manufacturers occupied the eastern half, and the Washington Market area on the west was taken up by food brokers of all kinds. For the New Yorkers who didn't do business in Tribeca, this downtown non-neighborhood was under the radar, busy during the day and deserted at night. Later, as factories and wholesale markets moved out of the area, many of the properties were turned over to dealers in electronic odds and ends, all operating in the shadow of the World Trade Center.

However, the architecture left behind was spectacular—magnificent cast-iron and brick buildings featuring spaces ripe for conversion by artists and other downtowners. In lightning-fast time, Tribeca became New York City's hippest new neighborhood, teeming with new bistros, bars, and clubs. But there are just a few excellent food shops.

Immediately to the south of Tribeca in the area around Wall Street food takes a back seat to finance. The Financial District, home to the Federal Reserve Bank, the New York Stock Exchange, and just about every other bank and trading house of importance, is dominated by business towers filled with office workers who retreat to the five boroughs after five o'clock, leaving the streets deserted, which explains the paucity of good food shops. But there is one culinary gem here that's definitely worth the trip, and we've included it here.

1. BOULEY BAKERY & MARKET

In the early 1980s, Tribeca was hardly an obvious location for a great restaurant. But David Bouley saw the neighborhood's potential and opened his restaurant on West Broadway to rave reviews. Bouley received four stars from the *New York Times,* and although the original closed in 1997 people still talk about the food. Today Bouley Bakery and Café is part of a complex that includes the new Bouley Restaurant, and Bouley Market. In summer the bakery is surrounded by small tables set behind glorious flower boxes, and a large pink flag with a white rabbit flutters above the store. Inside, a wood-burning oven works full-time, turning out breads and pastries. The excellent breads include garlic, a traditional French boule, and hazelnut. As for the pastries, the lemon tart, chocolate éclair, Dacquoise, and pastry puff filled with strawberry are amazing. Bouley Bakery also offers prepared food, soups, and sandwiches, with the daily menu written on a large slate wall. The ambience is charming at this lovely corner shop, where you'll be served with the easy grace that is a Bouley trademark.

2. CHRISTOPHER NORMAN CHOCOLATES

It's an odd location for a chocolate shop, tucked behind the security barriers next to the New York Stock Exchange, so odd that we annexed the Financial District's only food store of note to Tribeca, but that's where Christopher Norman Chocolates has thrived. Chef John Down originally trained as a painter, and the abstract paintings that inspire his chocolate creations decorate the shop. Down has brought his love of color to his artisanal craft, using pigment from vegetables and spices—saffron, wheat, black pepper, spinach, and cumin—to paint abstractions on chocolate. Down's flavors are daring and creative—green tea, arborio rice, curry, wild Italian cherry, and hibiscus stand out. His chocolate pears, with their subtle Pear William flavor, and gianduja chocolate truffles are also memorable. One of our favorites is a complete set of dark-chocolate dominoes, marked with white chocolate pips over a caramelized nougat center. You can watch Chef Down in the kitchen, painting chocolates with the intensity of a master. His show is much more captivating than the one right next door on the floor of the New York Stock Exchange.

3

BAZZINI

Finest Quality Since 1886

Quality Nuts • Dried Fruits
Fine Foods

CHEF PREPARED CUISINE
BREAKFAST
SANDWICHES • SALADS • PANINIS
DINNER
DESSERTS • ESPRESSO BAR
OLD FASHIONED SODA FOUNTAIN

WALK IN • TAKE OUT
GIFTS • BASKETS • BOXES • TINS
CATERING • SPECIAL EVENTS

www.bazzininuts.com

3

3. BAZZINI

Long before Tribeca sported its current name, Bazzini started as a nut-processing plant near the now-defunct Washington Market. Today, Bazzini is a neighborhood treasure, occupying a former warehouse space that has the feel and look of a large European covered market. The original columns and ceilings remain untouched, as do the black-and-white tile floors. Bazzini's nut bar features cashews, walnuts, pistachios, and several varieties of peanuts—honey-roasted, dry-roasted, shelled, and unshelled. The famous red, white, and blue Bazzini logo is emblazoned on everything from gigantic five-pound bags of pistachios to the excellent peanut butter. The grocery section features fresh produce, fruit, and cheese, all weighed on an old-fashioned market scale. An enormous salad bar occupies the center of the store, and countermen behind glass cases stand ready to make sandwiches and serve up prepared food to the lunchtime crowds of young financial guns and gurus.

SPICED NUT MIXTURE

BAZZINI / SERVES 6

While nuts are used as ingredients or garnishes in many recipes, this all-nut recipe is a good way to take advantage of Bazzini's bounteous selection. The great thing about this recipe is that it's only a theme. Every time you make this recipe, you can make it differently. Different spices, different quantities, different nuts—even the slightest change in ingredients makes this a surprise treat every time. Whatever the formula, this mixture is great with cocktails and a good reason to skip the hors d'oeuvres.

1 cup pistachios

1 cup pine nuts

1 cup almonds, blanched

¾ cup sugar

1 tablespoon honey

1 teaspoon ground cinnamon

½ teaspoon ground nutmeg

½ teaspoon very finely grated fresh ginger

Pinch of ground cayenne

1 Pour the nuts into a large nonstick skillet and set over medium-high heat.

2 In a bowl, mix together the sugar, honey, and 1 tablespoon water, pour the mixture over the nuts, and stir well.

3 In a separate bowl, mix together the cinnamon, nutmeg, ginger, and cayenne and add to the nuts.

4 Cook, stirring constantly, for 10 to 15 minutes, until the nuts are nicely browned and toasted.

5 Spread out on parchment or wax paper and let cool. Serve with apéritifs.

CHAPTER

4

GREENWICH VILLAGE

Greenwich Village was once a real village, a bucolic escape from the congestion of lower Manhattan. The Village has always been part of American cultural history: Thomas Paine, Henry James, Edith Wharton, Mark Twain, James Baldwin, Jack Kerouac, Edward Albee, Lenny Bruce, Janis Joplin, Woody Guthrie, and Woody Allen are just some of the artists who, at one time or another, lived and worked in this intimate part of downtown New York City.

In spite of its celebrities and a few touristy streets, the Village is still a peaceful enclave of large old trees, brick townhouses, small restaurants, and unique shops. Up until recently, the food scene in the Village was distinctly southern Italian: legendary butcher shops, bakeries, and grocers. The Village's bohemian coffeehouses started as neighborhood Italian cafés. But with the influx of new ethnic groups and a younger, demographic, the Village has become a truly international and trendy stop on the food trail. But in spite of the Village's high celebrity quotient, the food stores here are low-key and friendly with a strong neighborhood feel, very different than what you might expect from a place as famous as Greenwich Village.

1. OTTOMANELLI & SONS

Although many stores around New York City carry the Ottomanelli name, this butcher shop is the true original. Frank Ottomanelli has occupied this address for more than forty years. Ottomanelli's is famous citywide, if only for its unrivaled selection of wild game. This is the source for a few pounds of alligator or rattlesnake meat, both sold fresh. You'll also find ostrich steaks, kangaroo, venison, buffalo, antelope, and wild turkey. For those in a more traditional mood, the chicken and beef are excellent. But the next time you crave bear steak, call Frank, and he'll have one ready and waiting.

BRAISED BUFFALO SHORT RIBS
OTTOMANELLI & SONS / SERVES 6

About ten years ago, a group of innovative ranchers, responding to the demand for lower-fat meats, began to raise herds of the near depleted Great Plains bison, a.k.a. the American buffalo. The result is a tender, almost fatless meat, full of flavor. Here we put some of Ottomanelli's buffalo to work in a variation on a well-known dish. The object of braising is to make the meat so tender it falls off the bone. It's a two-step process: First the meat is seared over high heat, then it's slowly cooked in liquid..

1 cup flour

Salt and freshly ground black pepper

¼ cup olive oil

6 pounds buffalo short ribs, cut into single ribs

6 small onions, chopped

6 carrots, peeled and sliced

4 cloves garlic, chopped

1 teaspoon dried rosemary, crumbled

4 cups beef broth

¼ cup honey

1 Preheat the oven to 350 degrees.

2 Season the flour with salt and pepper, then dredge the ribs in the flour.

3 Heat the oil in a heavy ovenproof pot over medium-high heat and brown the short ribs in batches in a single layer. Do not crowd the pot or the beef will steam. Transfer the ribs to a platter and set aside.

4 Sauté the onions, carrots, garlic, and rosemary over medium heat until browned; season with salt and pepper to taste.

5 Add the broth, bring to a boil, and stir. Return the ribs to the pot in a single layer.

6 Cover and cook in the oven for 2 hours, or until the meat is almost falling off the bone.

7 Transfer the ribs to a platter.

8 Pour the liquid from the pot through a fine sieve set over a saucepan. Add the honey and bring to a boil; cook until the sauce thickens slightly. Pour the sauce over the ribs and serve.

2. DUFOUR PASTRY KITCHENS

The first thing you'll notice at Dufour is that it's difficult to get in. This wholesale pastry dough and hors d'oeuvres bakery sells primarily to the city's restaurants, with a limited retail business conducted mostly online. Don't let the guarded welcome throw you off: Once you use Dufour's pastry dough, you'll never bother to make your own again. The flaky French pâte feuilletée, ideal for Napoleons, vol-au-vents, or turnovers, bakes to a perfect consistency with a rich, buttery flavor. The dough keeps well in the freezer; just defrost two hours before you're ready to use. The tart shells come in several flavors, including chocolate, toasted almond, and cornmeal. Dufour's frozen hors d'oeuvres are simple and brilliant; our favorite is the mushroom truffle risotto. With your freezer filled with Dufour dough, tart shells, and hors d'oeuvres you'll be ready for cocktails for twenty or dinner for ten.

GOAT CHEESE TART

DUFOUR PASTRY / SERVES 6 AS AN APPETIZER

This simple appetizer using Dufour's puff pastry dough has rescued many an impromptu lunch.

1 package frozen Dufour puff pastry dough

1 (10-ounce) log goat cheese

1½ cups goat's milk

3 large eggs

Pinch of salt

Pinch of piment d'Espelette or ground cayenne

5 roasted red bell peppers, seeded, peeled, and cut in half lengthwise

¾ cup pine nuts

6 leaves fresh basil

1 Let the dough thaw, wrapped, for 1 to 2 hours.

2 Preheat the oven to 375 degrees.

3 Unwrap the dough and place it on a floured work surface.

4 Unfold the dough and roll it out to fit a 10-inch tart mold and fit the dough inside.

5 In a food processor, combine the goat cheese, goat's milk, eggs, salt, and piment d'Espelette.

6 Cover the bottom of the tart shell completely with one overlapping layer of roasted peppers. Sprinkle the pine nuts over the peppers.

7 Pour the goat cheese mixture into the tart shell. Bake for about 45 minutes, until a knife inserted in the center comes out clean. Garnish with the basil leaves and serve warm, with a large green salad.

3. MAGNOLIA BAKERY

There are visionaries even in the world of cupcakes. Alyssa Torey, founder of the Magnolia Bakery, is the Isaac Newton of her world. When Torey opened the Magnolia Bakery in 1996, no one else had a clue that cupcake love would sweep the country. But Torey converted a run-down Bleecker Street store into a pastel fantasy, and now lines of cupcake lovers stretching around the block wait patiently for her pink, blue, and yellow pastel wonders. The anatomy of the cupcake is simple: white or chocolate cake, covered in buttery pastel-colored frostings. But the simplest foods are often the hardest to make well, and Magnolia's attention to quality ingredients and fine detail make these cupcakes some of the best we've tried. But the Magnolia Bakery is not just about cupcakes. The thick-frosted full-sized layer cakes are real American comfort food, and don't miss the banana pudding, the Snickers icebox pie, and the caramel mini-cheesecake. Everything is baked from scratch in the store's ovens, then iced by hand before your eyes.

4. PORTO RICO IMPORTING COMPANY

It's a delight to discover Porto Rico Importing Company, purveyor and roaster of coffee beans since 1907. Before you even step inside, you'll smell the coffee. Porto Rico offers unblended coffees from South America, Central America, Africa, the Caribbean, India, Indonesia, and the Pacific. Multicolored burlap sacks of coffee beans and tins of tea line the floor and walls. Choose from twenty-two French roasts and twenty-six decaffeinated varieties, to name just two categories. The nearly infinite variety of blends can be confusing; as a start, we were intrigued by Swiss Chocolate, French Vanilla Bean, Tiramisù, DeCaf Strudel, and Double Nut Fudge. Porto Rico coffee is mixed in Williamsburg and brought to the store, fresh from the roaster. There's no place to sit in this tiny coffee haven—you won't find anybody hunched over a laptop. What you will find are great coffee blends to take home and savor.

5. BLUE RIBBON BAKERY & CAFE

The Blue Ribbon Bakery & Café is an intriguing hybrid of bakery and archaeological site. About ten years ago, the Bromberg brothers found an old brick oven in the basement of a closed bodega at the corner of Downing and Bedford Streets. The brothers, who trained at Le Cordon Bleu in France, restored the ancient oven and soon after opened Blue Ribbon Bakery. The offerings here include freshly baked bread and all sorts of condiments, including honey produced in Mexico exclusively for Blue Ribbon. Among the spice mixtures, the Perfect Roast blend for chicken and beef is outstanding. The atmosphere at Blue Ribbon is youthful, friendly, and fun. Even if you're not sitting down at the restaurant, you can order one of their sandwiches, made on the massive marble counter. Try the yellowfin tuna on toasted challah or the Blue Ruben—chorizo, coleslaw, and Cheddar on a baguette.

6. MYERS OF KESWICK

Myers of Keswick, a small shop on Hudson Street not far from the White Horse Tavern, is a perfect replica of an English village grocer, circa 1935. Keswick is a small Cornwall village, and the store bills itself as "That Bastion of Albion in Manhattan." You enter the shop through a wooden screen door on squeaky springs. The decor is so convincing that you would be only mildly surprised if Jeeves came by, looking for a can of Morton's Mushy Peas or a packet of loose tea from Taylor's at Harrowgate. Keswick's keen sense of kitsch goes straight to the Queen Elizabeth dishtowels. On one side, you'll see neat stacks of English canned and packaged foods, mostly beans and teas. On the other side, on the white-enameled butcher counter, you'll find pies and sausages—pork pies, sausage rolls, and Cornish pasties made here by Myers and sold under its English Glory label. The steak and kidney pie is good enough to convince at least one Frenchwoman that English cooking, in fact, has some merit. Stop into Keswick's, pick up some bangers and kidney pie, and discover that you don't have to be born in the U.K. to appreciate English food.

7. MURRAY'S CHEESE

We've never met an Italian named Murray, but local lore has it that Murray's, New York's best cheese shop, opened in 1940 as a conventional Italian grocery. In 1960 when Rob Kaufelt, the current owner, bought the store cheese, for most Americans, came in one color and one shape: yellow and square. "Real" cheese was considered an affectation, a fancy food for people who spoke French, and more often than not was smelly, gooey, and not always yellow. But Kaufelt, a true believer in the power of cheese, fought back against this deep cultural resistance. One of the secrets behind his success is the basement cheese cave. To age the cheese properly and deliver the best possible taste, cheese must be stored at precisely the right temperature and humidity. Before Murray's, most imported cheeses were badly stored and rendered funky, flat, and lifeless. Kaufelt believed that he could convert the masses by getting them to taste cheese the way it was meant to be tasted. New Yorkers discovered Murray's, and thus began their love affair with cheese. The first thing you'll notice in Murray's sparkling shop is the row of cheese refrigerators. There you'll find all 250 varieties: goat's milk, sheep, cow, buffalo. Cheese from France: Fromage de Meaux, Camembert de Bocage, and Epoisse. From Italy: Capra Valtellina and Castelrosso. From Spain: Cabra al Vino and Queso de la Serena. These are just a few of the wonderful cheeses from only three of the fourteen countries represented. If you find this massive selection daunting the manager will be more than happy to enlighten you about any cheese in the case, cutting you a few samples along the way. Coming from nowhere cheesewise, today Murray's holds its own with the best cheese stores in the world.

8. JACQUES TORRES

The charismatic Jacques Torres combines an impeccable sense of style with total mastery of the art of making chocolate. He is, in his way, the splendid progeny of Milton Hershey and Coco Chanel. Torres started his career as a pastry chef and quickly became a star. He was the youngest to win the Meilleur Ouvrier de France. Torres put in a long stint at Le Cirque in New York, created a television series for PBS, and wrote several cookbooks. In 2001 he left the restaurant business to follow his real passion, chocolate, opening Jacques Torres Chocolates in Brooklyn's Dumbo. Jacques Torres's new Manhattan store, Chocolate Haven, is a marvel of technology and elegance. Torres has designed an unusual duo—an impeccable chocolate factory matched by a charming shop. But the real revelation is the chocolate. Torres uses only natural ingredients with no preservatives or additives. Cacao beans come to Chocolate Haven from around the world, to be roasted and refined in the factory. The chocolate shapes are traditional, but the tastes are superior and unusual: Fresh Squeezed Lemon and Raspberry Lemon were among our favorites. You can buy by the piece or choose from prepackaged assortments of light and dark chocolates. And do not miss the wonderful hot chocolate. Making great chocolate is a subtle art, and Jacques Torres is a master.

9. FAICCO'S PORK

Bleecker Street was once lined with pushcarts selling fruits, vegetables, bread, and other basics for the home cupboard. When Joseph Faicco opened this store in 1950 he couldn't afford refrigeration so he restocked the sausage every morning, in the process earning a reputation for making the freshest pork sausage on the block. Faicco's habit of making sausage fresh daily continues to the present. Early each morning the kitchen crew grinds pork, adds seasonings, and stuffs that day's supply of sausages. The truth is that Faicco has to make sausage fresh every day because, by day's end, it's completely sold out. You can choose hot or sweet, with or without garlic, cheese, fennel, or parsley. Try the sweet fennel-flavored pork sausage, excellent in a marinara over penne pasta.

FAICCO'S TENDER PORK CUTLETS

FAICCO'S PORK / SERVES 4

This recipe lets the quality of Faicco's pork shine through, with just enough flavoring to add interest but not enough to mask the delicate fresh taste of these succulent cutlets. It's quick and simple, a good demonstration of how quality ingredients and careful preparation can make all the difference.

2 medium eggs

3 tablespoons milk

½ teaspoon salt

Pinch of freshly ground black pepper

1 cup bread crumbs

1½ pounds Faicco's boneless pork cutlets

½ cup extra-virgin olive oil

2 tablespoons chopped fresh parsley

1 Beat the eggs and milk in a bowl and set aside. In a separate bowl, combine the salt, pepper, and bread crumbs.

2 One at a time, dip the pork cutlets in the egg mixture, then dredge in the bread crumb mixture and place on a plate.

3 When all the cutlets are coated, heat the oil in a frying pan over medium heat until a bit of bread crumbs dropped into the oil sizzles immediately, add the cutlets, and cook for around 5 minutes on each side, until lightly browned.

4 Drain the cutlets on paper towels, garnish with parsley, and serve hot with a green salad.

10. CHOCOLATE BAR

After visiting a half dozen specialty chocolate shops we thought there couldn't possibly be a new way to sell chocolate. Alison Nelson's Chocolate Bar proved us wrong. The bright blue storefront and playful retro '70s decor give the first inklings that things were different here. Alison Nelson works with some of the city's finest chocolate makers to offer her West Village customers a fantastic variety of chocolate treats. The chocolates get high marks for originality of design and flavor—Pumpkin Spice, Port Wine, and Wicked Hot are just a few. The Chocolate Bar also features reworked "retro classics," like PB&C (peanut butter and milk chocolate filled with caramel), and the Elvis (layers of banana, marshmallow, and caramel wrapped in a graham crust and dipped in chocolate). The Atomic collection features the Black-and-White, sumptuous layers of marshmallow, chocolate, and graham crust. The owners call this a candy store for grown-ups, and everything about the Chocolate Bar is fun, from the people behind the bar to the music they play. Finally, don't miss the creamy, thick hot chocolate, the hot liquid caramel, and the chocolate-dipped pretzels.

CHOCOLATE MARTINI
CHOCOLATE BAR / SERVES 1

"A chocolate martini is not a serious drink," according to Alison Nelson, the founder of Chocolate Bar. "It is strictly a fun concoction, specially blended for parties and lighthearted socializing. This recipe is easy enough for the home mixologist and swank enough for the discerning martini drinker." The Chocolate Bar's excellent cocoa powder adds a special zing to any chocolate recipe.

½ teaspoon Dutch process cocoa powder

½ teaspoon sugar

1½ shots chocolate liqueur

1½ shots crème de cacao

½ shot vanilla-flavored vodka

2½ shots half-and-half

1 Mix together the cocoa powder and sugar.

2 Rim a chilled martini glass with water and dip it into the sugar and cocoa mixture.

3 Combine the chocolate liqueur, crème de cacao, vodka, and half-and-half in a cocktail shaker with ice and shake well.

4 Strain into the prepared glass.

retro
CARAMEL APPLE
premium milk chocolate filled with apple flavored caramel

retro
SALTY PRETZEL
premium dark chocolate with salty pretzel chunks

chocolate bar

NET WT. 2.25 OZ(64G)

PURE NOSTALGIA. GREAT CHOCOLATE.

48

ZAGAT
RATED

huh? what?
How 'Bout This
CRAZY WEATHER
y'?
hmm... Minty Mocha
spicy hot chocolate
vanilla cocoa tea
classic buzzed
hot chocolate

10

11. FLORENCE MEAT MARKET

Florence is the butcher shop that many New Yorkers consider their own personal secret. How many times have we been collared by someone who told us, "There's a tiny butcher shop off the map in the Village that sells aged prime meat at insanely low prices"? Florence is amazing, but it's no longer a secret: Most Villagers know that Florence is a contender for the title of best butcher in the city. The beef here is prime Angus, dry-aged on the premises for more than three weeks. One of the specialties is Newport Steak, a strip steak cut from the sirloin, less chewy than rump steak and less fatty than a short loin strip. Florence has an old-time feel, with sawdust on the floor and a meat locker with a big wooden door. The owner, Benny Pizzuco, is a master butcher, as ample as his shop, and his helpers couldn't be friendlier. When we met Pizzuco he was working behind the counter on another specialty—veal shoulder, great for blanquette de veau, braised veal shoulder, or a simple veal stew.

11

GIGOT DE SEPT HEURES

FLORENCE MEAT MARKET / SERVES 6

When we told Pizzuco this recipe for slow-cooked leg of lamb, he asked to be invited to dinner and then cut us a perfectly proportioned leg of lamb, one of the tenderest and most flavorful we've ever had. In France gigot de sept heures, or seven-hour leg of lamb, is an Easter favorite reserved for holidays, but everyone in the family knows it's even better the next day.

5- to 6-pound leg of lamb, with bone

⅓ cup olive oil

½ cup rum

5 large carrots, peeled and cut into large chunks

1 whole celery stalk, finely chopped

1 fennel bulb, finely chopped

20 whole shallots, peeled

5 pieces orange zest

¼ cup sugar

Salt and freshly ground black pepper to taste

1 Bring a large casserole of water to a boil over high heat, then add the leg of lamb, making sure it's completely covered with water, and boil for 5 minutes; remove from the water and pat dry. Discard the water.

2 Heat the oil in the casserole over high heat, add the leg of lamb, and brown it, turning it to brown all sides.

3 Pour the rum over the lamb and use a long match or a lighter to ignite the rum.

4 Reduce the heat to low, add the carrots, celery, fennel, shallots, and orange zest. Cook, covered, over low heat, turning the lamb every hour, for 6 hours.

5 Uncover the casserole, add the sugar, and cook, uncovered, over very low heat for 1 more hour. Carefully remove the meat and vegetables to a platter. If the sauce is too thin, cook over high heat until it is reduced and thickened. Add salt and pepper to taste and serve immediately with roasted potatoes.

11

ALLEVA
MIDWOOD
633-7200
OVER 100 YEARS
ALLEVA
PROSCIUTTO - SOPRESSATA
188 - RICOTTA
SANDWICHES
PANINI
TONY'S LITTLE
GIFT SHOP
CITTERIO
Alleva
BEST QUALITY
FILIPPO BERIO
OLIVE OIL
EXTRA VIRGIN
GENUINE FULVI
PRODUCT OF ITALY
DOPE IS
FOR DOPES
DON'T BE
A DOPE!

CHAPTER 5 LITTLE ITALY

The Little Italy of great restaurants, passionate people, and tough customers is a neighborhood in transition. Though many of the original immigrant families have moved to the outer boroughs and suburbs, you can still see old men on their folding chairs in front of tenement buildings while, above them, old women lean on windowsills, pillows beneath their arms. But these days they're not watching kids play stickball in the street; they're watching an endless stream of the young, the trendy, and the beautiful.

Walking Mott and Mulberry Streets, you can hear tour guides call out the holy sites of pop culture: "This is where *The Godfather* was filmed. This is where Joey Gallo was shot." You can even take the Sopranos tour. Many of the original businesses are gone or have been theme-parked beyond all recognition, but the neighborhood still maintains a scaled-down charm. At one time, Little Italy was home to thousands of immigrants from southern Italy, and the food stores and restaurants still exude that distinctive Neapolitan or Sicilian flavor. To add to that flavor, every September 19 a statue of Saint Gennaro, the principal patron saint of Naples, is taken from its permanent place in the Church of Most Precious Blood on Mulberry Street and carried in joyous procession through the streets of Little Italy. The weeklong Festival of San Gennaro is not to be missed. Booths offering everything from sausages and onions to "Kiss me I'm Italian" T-shirts line the gaudily lit streets. For a brief moment every year these few blocks of downtown Manhattan look and feel like Naples. But whenever you go to Little Italy, look closely and you will find wonderful food stores with authentic character and quality.

1. DESPANA

There are plenty of bodegas in Manhattan, but only Despaña sells food products exclusively from Spain. Despaña is Andalusian right down to the fighting bull's head mounted on the wall over the counter; it's the head of a bull killed by El Cordobes. Judging from the head, the rest of that bull was the size of a small truck. Despaña is done up like a trendy Madrid tapaseria—wood floors, marble countertops, and a small open kitchen. Here you can pick up one of Despaña's homemade chorizo, including chorizo picante, cantimpalo, and the ultimate chorizo iberico made from Iberian pork. Their Serrano ham is cured for more than a year, giving it a deep, rich flavor. Try the ham in a bocadillo, a spicier version of the panini. Despaña also is the place to learn about the less well known but superb Spanish cheeses. Order a "flight" from their cheese case—iberico con tres leches, Manchego, Torta del Casar, Murcio al Vino, Queso de Cantabria, Queso de la Serena—and you will be convinced that the Spanish rank among the world's great cheese makers. Across from the serving counters, choose from the shelves of packaged Spanish products. If you want to make a perfect paella, Despaña is the place to pick up Spanish rice, squid ink, and saffron. Don't leave without canned belly of tuna—the best part of the tuna and the best tuna out of a can you've ever tasted.

TORTILLA

DESPAÑA / SERVES 3

The tortilla, one of the traditional dishes of Spain, is eaten at breakfast, lunch, or dinner and often served cut into little pieces as tapas. Think of it as a Spanish frittata, or omelette paysan. This tortilla, made with ingredients from Despaña, can be served warm with a green salad or cold in a sandwich.

3 large russet or Yukon Gold potatoes, peeled and cut into 1-inch pieces

½ cup olive oil

2 large eggs

Salt and freshly ground black pepper

1 large onion, diced

1 Dry the sliced potatoes on a paper towel.

2 Heat the oil with the potatoes in a 9-inch nonstick frying pan over low heat and cook until the potatoes are tender inside but not browned.

3 In a large bowl, beat the eggs until foamy, then season with salt and pepper.

4 Drain the potatoes and add them to the eggs.

5 Discard the excess oil in the pan and, in the same pan, fry the onion over medium heat until softened, 15 to 20 minutes. Pour off any excess oil and place the pan over medium heat.

6 Pat the onions dry and add them to the potato mixture.

7 Pour the mixture into the pan and cook for 5 minutes, flattening the tortilla with a wooden spoon.

8 Flip the tortilla by holding a large plate over the pan, inverting it, and sliding the tortilla back into the pan; cook for 5 more minutes. Remove from the pan and slice.

2. CECI-CELA

The window sign here reads "La patisserie des connosiers," and though these pastry chefs may not know how to spell connoisseurs, they do know how to bake for them. The pastry case in this long, narrow store is filled with the croissants, tartes sucrées, financiers, and mille-feuilles that, year after year, put Ceci-Cela at the top of nearly every pastry poll in New York City. A Parisian bus stop sign stands at the entrance of Ceci-Cela; you definitely will have to queue up for your chocolate éclairs. But what éclairs!

3. CIAO BELLA GELATO

Jon Snyder, the unofficial Emperor of (Italian) Ice Cream, started Ciao Bella Gelato when he was still a high school student. Twenty years ago, Snyder sold the company to a new management company, which turned the boutique label into a national brand. This is still Ciao Bella's flagship store, its exterior decorated by neighborhood artists and "tagged" by local graffiti greats. You can mark the seasons here by the size of the crowd; in summer, the sidewalk is packed. Ciao Bella is real gelato, the recipe imported from Torino. Try the hazelnut biscotti gelato, and the blood orange or raspberry mango sorbet. The cookie sandwich, a slab of gelato squeezed between two homemade cookies, is a standout.

4. DELIMANJOO

Delimanjoo is a franchise that makes delicious Korean fast food. The custard cakes here are made by a robotic machine that looks like an escapee from a car factory. Light vanilla cake on the outside and creamy custard on the inside, Delimanjoo custard cakes are made in corny molds to look like little ears of corn. These fresh-baked Korean variations on the madeleine are delicious. It's easy to eat a dozen at time.

5. ALBANESE MEATS & POULTRY

On Mott Street between Prince and Houston, you'll first see several elegant shops devoted to home design, jewelry, and men's custom tailoring. Across the street from these high-end emporia is a crumbling red brick storefront with a faded cardboard turkey glued to one window. The sign above the windows, hand-lettered in black, reads "Albanese Meats & Poultry." Behind the white enamel display case, next to their chopping blocks, stand two butchers at the ready with cleavers and knives. Albanese is a very old-school butcher shop. These butchers cut, trim, and sell meat. That's it. The service is quick and professional, the meat fresh and well cut. Buy a roast here and you'll be doing your part to preserve a neighborhood treasure.

6. RICE TO RICHES

The upscale food world behaves a lot like the fashion business. Trends change quickly: If "red is the new black," then rice pudding is this year's flourless chocolate cake. That's one way to explain how a store entirely devoted to rice pudding not only survives but thrives. Rice to Riches, which looks like a Star Trek set, is packed with customers day and night. Even if you don't like rice pudding, a quick read of the dozen-plus flavors makes the trip worthwhile: Sex, Drugs, and Rocky Road; Secret Life of Pumpkin; Stubborn Banana; Rest in Peach—all these can be enhanced with such evocative toppings as Logic, Heart Throb, and Chocolate Chip Flirt.

5

6

7. ALLEVA DAIRY

Alleva is one of Little Italy's last remaining mozzarella makers. The store, run by the fourth and fifth generations of the Alleva family, has been in business for more than one hundred years. In Italy there's a latteria in just about every village, but handmade mozzarella is getting harder and harder to find in New York, and the difference between handmade and the stuff made by machine is like the difference between Camembert and Velveeta. Alleva makes mozzarella fresh every morning and delivers the cheese to restaurants all over the city. The day begins with curds, made fresh from whole or skim milk. The curds are mixed with fresh milk in a large steaming jar, then shaped by hand into a white ball before being set to cure in a vat of cold water, salted or unsalted. Alleva still displays its antique gilded glass signs advertising "Burro e uova" (butter and eggs) and "Latticini di Nostra Produzione" (mozzarella and fresh ricotta made here).

LASAGNA

ALLEVA DAIRY / SERVES 4

Lasagna is a much maligned Italian dish, mostly because it's been done so badly by so many mediocre restaurants. Try this recipe with Alleva ricotta and discover why lasagna got famous in the first place. This traditional lasagna can feed a family for weeks. One slice is a complete meal.

1 (16-ounce) package dried lasagna noodles

4 cups Alleva ricotta

¼ cup freshly grated Parmesan cheese

4 large eggs

2 cups shredded Alleva mozzarella cheese

1 Preheat the oven to 350 degrees.

2 Bring a large pot of salted water to a boil. Add the noodles and cook for 8 to 10 minutes, or until almost done. Drain and lay the lasagna flat on a piece of aluminum foil to cool.

3 In a medium bowl, combine the ricotta, Parmesan, eggs and mix well.

4 Spread ½ cup of the ricotta mixture in the bottom of a 9-by-13-inch baking dish.

5 Cover with a layer of noodles. Spread half the remaining ricotta mixture over the noodles; top with another noodle layer. Spread 1½ cups of the ricotta mixture over the noodles.

6 Top with the remaining noodles and ricotta mixture and sprinkle mozzarella over all.

7 Cover with greased foil and bake for 45 minutes, or until the top is golden.

8. DI PALO'S DAIRY

On Broome Street, you can now find Italian grocery stores that sell sushi. At Di Palo's salumeria you won't find a trace of toro. What you will see: huge stacked wheels of Parmesan and enormous hanging bulbs of Asiago gently aging in the natural light of the store windows. Inside you will find an enormous selection of Italian cheeses, oil, vinegar, and packaged foods. Be prepared to wait: Customers take numbers from a machine, and it's not unusual to find yourself twenty numbers down the list. At Di Palo's the wait is so long because the service is so good. The counterman will insist you try several kinds of each cheese or olive oil before you make your choice. Lou Di Palo, whose great-grandfather founded the store, scours the Italian countryside for anything new that strikes his eye and his palate—olive oils from obscure farms, and a selection of balsamic vinegars, including one aged for over one hundred years. Lou knows every producer by name and can tell you the exact quality of the air, soil, and water that gave birth to your olives, pimentos, or canned tomatoes. He will also tell you about St. Eustachio coffee, slowly roasted on wood for sweetness, the kind of Roman coffee that makes perfect cappuccino. If you are here on Friday or Saturday, stand in line for the creamy burrata mozzarella just flown in from Rome and sold out within hours of arrival. Di Palo and family work very hard to keep things Italian in Little Italy.

DI PALO'S FAMOUS CHEESECAKE

DI PALO'S DAIRY / SERVES 6 TO 8

The Di Palo family's secret cheesecake recipe is no longer secret. Lou Di Palo was good enough to share this recipe with us. It may take a few tries before you get everything exactly right—making cheesecake is as much about touch as it is about ingredients—but this recipe is well worth the effort. Be sure you have a few friends around to share it with, or you might be tempted to eat the whole cheesecake.

Butter for the pan

½ cup grated zwieback toast

1½ cups sugar

3 pounds Di Palo ricotta

6 large eggs

1 teaspoon vanilla extract

4 teaspoons orange flower water

¾ cup heavy cream

2 tablespoons lemon zest

1 Preheat the oven to 350 degrees.

2 Butter the bottom of a 9-inch springform pan.

3 Mix the zwieback with ½ cup of the sugar. Coat the bottom and sides of the pan with this mixture, pressing up the sides with your fingers.

4 Mix together the ricotta, remaining sugar, eggs, vanilla, orange flower water, cream, and lemon zest. Pour the mixture into the prepared pan.

5 Bake for 1 hour, until the edges are slightly browned but the center still quivers slightly.

9

8

9

9. PIEMONTE RAVIOLI

Security at Piemonte Ravioli is tight. Only family members are allowed in the kitchen. They have guarded their secret pasta recipe since 1920. Such vigilance is justified. The store's brochure, printed daily, lists forty-eight different kinds of pasta—fresh, dry, and frozen—and three sizes of ravioli in multiple flavors. Lately Piemonte has added homemade sauces: Bolognese, pesto, puttanesca, amatriciana. Many stores in Little Italy have undergone cosmetic surgery, but this little store has aged gracefully. Nothing fancy here, just good storemade tortellini, cannelloni, ravioli, and stuffed shells.

10. WINE THERAPY

Let's say you want a glass of organic wine while you're having your hair done, or you want to shop for antiques while tasting a Pinot Noir from a small Oregon producer. Wine Therapy is your place. It all started as Tricia Kirkland's hair salon, Tricia's Place, then her husband, Jean Baptiste, moved into the space next door and opened Wine Therapy, a wine store dedicated to small organic producers from around the world. They then decorated the store with antiques, all of which are for sale. The décor is very cool, the wines are unusual and very interesting, and the hairstyling is excellent.

MELON SOUP

WINE THERAPY / SERVES 4

This is a great summer starter course with the best compliments-to-labor ratio of any soup we've ever made. It takes about ten minutes to whip up, and your guests will be talking about it all night. One reason is that it really is delicious; the other is the alcohol content. Don't forget to tell your guests there's wine in the soup or they'll be wondering why the room is spinning.

4 cantaloupes

1 cup Muscat wine

½ lemon

Freshly ground black pepper

1   Cut 3 of the cantaloupes in half and remove the seeds with a spoon.

2   Scoop out the flesh and puree it in a blender until smooth.

3   Add the wine and squeeze the lemon half over the puree.

4   Add pepper to taste, being careful to taste as you go.

5   Cut the remaining cantaloupe in half and scoop out the seeds. Cut the flesh into small chunks and divide equally among 4 bowls.

6   Pour the soup over the cantaloupe chunks and refrigerate for 3 hours before serving.

10

ONAH SHIMMEL
KNISH BAKERY
The Original
YONAH SCHIMMEL
KNISHERY
Special
BAKERS DOZEN
FROM
YONAH SCHIMMEL
KNISHES
RENT
5578
137

CHAPTER 6
LOWER EAST SIDE

Just across Houston Street from the East Village is the Lower East Side. The Lower East Side is, for many Americans, a Jewish homeland second only to Israel. This is where the great waves of Jewish immigration from central Europe came ashore, where the garment industry was born, where some of New York's oldest synagogues still stand, and where you will find New York's most famous Jewish food stores: pickle factories, pastrami makers, bakers, and delicatessens. Third- and fourth-generation Jewish families still come into Manhattan from suburbia to show their kids the wonders of Katz's Deli, where, during World War II, the battle cry was "Send a salami to your boy in the Army." In the 1950s and '60s the Lower East Side absorbed waves of immigration from Puerto Rico and the Dominican Republic. And more recently, a new generation of food pioneers looking to escape the high rents of Soho, Nolita, and Tribeca has moved into the Lower East Side, opening edgy new stores and adding new flavor to the already rich culinary landscape. The old tenements are slowly being refurbished into high-rent homes for young professionals, and Essex and Ludlow Streets are now lined with innovative restaurants and food stores.

1. RUSS & DAUGHTERS

"I'm going to the appetizing" is pure New York-ese for a store that sells smoked fish, caviar, cheese, and other Eastern European delicacies. Without question, the most appetizing of these stores is Russ & Daughters, in the business since 1904. A third generation of the Russ family opened the Houston Street store in 1940. The original neon sign seems lifted from an Edward Hopper painting. As you enter Russ & Daughters, you are welcomed into another world. The white enamel counters and cases are pristine dioramas for the sparkling array of delicacies: fresh sturgeon, sable, whitefish, and chubs. The salads—whitefish, shrimp, smoked salmon, and lobster—mixed with homemade mayonnaise, a touch of celery, herbs, and spices. Battalions of smoked salmon from Gaspé and Scotland, Canada and California arrayed in strict formation catch the eye. A complex mix of scents teases the appetite: the pungent North Sea smell of pickled herring, the oaky mist of smoked fish. The service at Russ & Daughters rivals the food. Behind the counters, the men in starched coats and white paper hats deftly cut translucent slices from sides of salmon. Every smiling counterman has a different story—usually long and sometimes funny. You'll get your fish impeccably trimmed along with a few laughs, some local gossip, and a taste thrown in for free. If you want to start a new ritual, head to Russ & Daughters on December 31 and join the blocklong line of loyal customers, waiting patiently in the cold for the chance to buy a few ounces of New Year's caviar.

CHOPPED CHICKEN LIVER

RUSS & DAUGHTERS / SERVES 8 TO 10

For an older generation of New Yorkers the expression "What am I, chopped liver?" meant "Stop ignoring me. I'm important too." But this delicious chopped liver will not lack for attention. Serve on matzo or crackers.

1 pound fresh chicken livers

4 tablespoons unsalted butter

2 large onions, peeled and chopped

3 large hard-cooked eggs, chilled

Kosher salt and freshly ground pepper

1   Drain the livers, rinse them, and pat them dry. Remove any connective tissue.

2   Heat 2 tablespoons of the butter in a large skillet over medium heat and sauté the livers until they are firm but still slightly pink in the center, about 5 minutes. Remove with a slotted spoon and place on a plate to cool. Reserve the cooking juices.

3   In a clean, large skillet, melt the remaining butter over medium heat and add the onions. Sauté until the onions are caramelized, 30 to 40 minutes, reducing the heat to low as the onions soften.

4   When the onions are ready, coarsely chop the livers in a food processor and place in a bowl. Peel the eggs and mash them with a fork in a bowl. Add to the livers.

5   Add the onions and mix well, stirring in just enough of the cooking juices to moisten the mixture. Season with salt and pepper to taste.

6   Cover the chopped liver and let mellow in the refrigerator for at least a few hours. Remove from the refrigerator 15 minutes before serving.

2

2. STREIT'S MATZO

Matzo is the Hebrew name for the unleavened flatbread made by the people of the Exodus. At first eaten only during Passover, many have adopted matzo as a crisp, tasty replacement for ordinary crackers, great with cream cheese or dipped in hummus. For Jewish families, matzo is the lead ingredient in traditional foods like matzo ball soup, matzo brei (a matzo and egg omelet), and matzo kugel (a matzo-based pudding). Streit's matzo factory on Rivington Street, opened in 1925, ships thousands of pounds around the world every week. Traditionally, matzo was made by hand from flour and water, then left to dry in the sun. At Streit's factory, matzo is pressed at high speed through gleaming silver rollers, then baked, dried, and then packed in an exquisitely timed matzo gavotte.

GRANDMA ROSE'S MATZO BREI
STREIT'S MATZO / SERVES 4 TO 6

This traditional Passover treat is named after Susan's grandmother, a legendary cook. Matzo brei, redolent of childhood memories, is a sort of Jewish tortilla, using matzo instead of potatoes. It's great for breakfast or brunch.

8 pieces matzo

4 large eggs

2 cups milk

1 teaspoon kosher salt

½ cup (1 stick) unsalted butter

1 Break the matzo into 1- to 2-inch squares and put in a large bowl.

2 In a separate bowl, beat the eggs, milk, and salt together, then pour the mixture over the matzo and toss to coat. Let the matzo soak for about 20 minutes, until the matzo is softened but not soggy.

3 Melt the butter in a large frying pan over medium heat and pour in the matzo mixture; when the matzo starts to brown, toss with a spatula, turning the mixture until all the matzo is a golden brown color. Serve hot, for breakfast or a late-night snack with sugar or your favorite jam or even maple syrup.

3. YONAH SCHIMMEL

Well before fast food, there was Yonah Schimmel's knishery, founded in 1910. The knish is a handheld Jewish dumpling, a pierogi offshoot, with a thin, doughy skin wrapped around a soft filling, usually potato or kasha (buckwheat), or sometimes spinach, and then steamed or grilled until smoking hot. In Eastern Europe, knishes were quite small, but in New York they've evolved to the size of a shotput and are often just as heavy. But at Yonah Schimmel the knishes are pillowy froths of flavor surrounded by a delicate pastry skin. Buy a few boxes of knishes to freeze at home or, better yet, take a few to the small eating space in the back. You'll be amused by photos of long-dead knish-loving celebrities and the homemade ads—"Send a Knish to Your Mother in Florida." A black-and-white television runs all day, looking like it might, at any minute, pick up the 1956 variety shows. With the resurgence of the Lower East Side, you'll see locals grabbing a knish on their way to an indie film at the Sunshine Theater down the block.

4. BABYCAKES NYC

Erin McKenna founded Babycakes to spread her deeply held gospel—"Everyone needs cupcakes, even people with food allergies." A born cupcake lover, McKenna is allergic to wheat and dairy and doesn't eat refined sugar. So she created her own line of cakes and cookies free from eggs, wheat, dairy products, nuts, casein, soy, refined sugar, and gluten. While a good cupcake seems out of reach given this long list of no-no's, McKenna has assembled new ingredients for her "gentle treats for delicate tummies"—virgin cold-pressed coconut oil, agave nectar and date sugar, two sweeteners so low on the glycemic index that they're suitable for diabetics. Lest this sound too technical, McKenna's party-colored cupcakes are so pretty and so good you don't need a food allergy to love them.

5. DELANCEY LIVE CHICKEN

This Asian butcher shop is not for the faint of heart. Here customers can choose a bird from a flock of live chickens, ducks, and pigeons and have it slaughtered, cleaned, and dressed on the spot. Most of the patrons at Delancey Live are recent arrivals from China, but the store has been discovered by trendy "foodies" and was recently featured in *Vogue* magazine. The specialty at Delancey Live is Silky chicken, a white feathered Chinese with deep black skin and meat. Cooked, Silky chicken is extraordinarily intense and flavorful. If you can't work up the courage to go inside Delancey Live Chicken, look for the remarkable chicken mural that graces its front wall. It is the finest chicken mural in all of Manhattan.

6. ECONOMY CANDY

Imagine a candy store run by Daffy Duck's less organized brother. Starting in 1937, Economy has made it its business to carry just about every type of commercial candy (ever) made. Challenging in a shopping mall, in Economy's tiny space, it's a miracle of organized chaos. The shelves of glass jars filled with Mary Janes, Red Hots, Tootsie Pops, Pez, Turkish Taffy, Atomic Fireballs, Goobers, Dubble Bubble, Jawbreakers, Sugar Babies, Sugar Daddies, Necco Wafers, Jujubes, Good & Plenty, and Black Jack Gum (yes, it's black) stack straight up to the stamped tin ceiling. You'll also see halvah, Jordan almonds, bubble gum cigars, chocolate cigarettes, sour balls, gumdrops, jelly beans, and those candy buttons on white paper strips. And more. The shelves are precariously balanced, tons of candy on the verge of tumbling down at any moment. At Economy Candy, with its vast selection of treats from everyone's childhood, even an amnesiac could wax nostalgic.

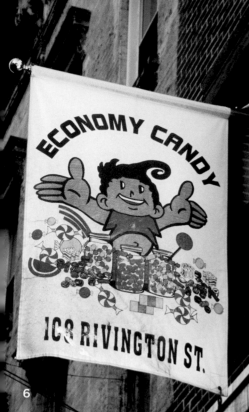

6

6

4

10

GUSS PICKLES

THREE GENERATIONS OF QUALITY

SERVING NEW YORK SINCE 1920

9

9

9

8

8

8

7. KOSSAR'S BIALYS

Most people have never seen or eaten a bialy, a chewy yeast roll covered with onions. It has its origins in the Jewish community of Bialystok, about a hundred miles northwest of Warsaw. That community was destroyed in the Holocaust, but the tradition of the bialystoker kuchen goes on and today Kossar's makes the best bialys anywhere. The dough, or tagelach—made of high-gluten flour, yeast, and water—is molded by hand into the bialy's distinctive saucer shape, then coated with onion paste made from freshly cut onions. The raw bialys bake on wooden "peels" in a special brick oven for seven minutes. Always buy bialys hot, and always buy them at Kossar's.

8. DOUGHNUT PLANT

Mark Israel started his doughnut business with a family recipe he found by chance among his grandfather's papers. With no money to rent space, he began making small batches in the basement of his Lower East Side tenement. He delivered his doughnuts by bicycle to a few sympathetic local coffee shops. But these were no ordinary crullers; these were the masterworks of a doughnut virtuoso. Before long, orders overwhelmed capacity, and in 1984 Israel started the Doughnut Plant. At the Doughnut Plant, things start cooking just as the most devoted night birds are heading home. The expert team of bakers mixes batches of all-natural batter, then hand-cuts the dough into doughnut shapes. Set aside to rise for an hour, the doughnuts then go for a short dip in the fryer. Israel uses chopsticks to turn the doughnuts in the fryer, then carefully places each one on a wire rack. He repeats the process for forty different flavors, about two thousand doughnuts daily.

9. GUSS'S PICKLES

Everyone knows that New York is the financial capital of the world. How many know that, in the eighteenth century, New York was the cucumber capital? Actually, Brooklyn was the cucumber capital, but the cucumbers were ferried to Manhattan to be made into pickles. Because pickles keep well without refrigeration, they became a staple for poor immigrant families. At one time, there were more than one hundred pickle stores in New York City; today there is Guss's Pickles on Orchard Street. Dozens of brilliant red barrels crowd the sidewalk in front, filled to the brim with pickles. Their briny aroma fills the street. Guss's pickles are crisp, cold, and palate-cleansing, with an aftertaste of peppercorn, juniper, and dill. But it's not all pickled cucumbers here. Try the sauerkraut, peppers (sweet or hot), capers, mushrooms, green tomatoes, and artichokes. The original Guss sold his store in the 1970s. The new owners have inherited Guss's passion for pickles, follow all the old recipes, and, of course, cherish his trademark red barrels.

10. GERTEL'S BAKERY

Challah is a braided Jewish bread reserved for the Sabbath or for holidays, but, as many people know, challah is also a great everyday bread. Like many challah bakeries, Gertel's bakes its beautifully glazed, hand-plaited egg and honey breads right in the store. What sets Gertel's challahs apart is their size—world-record size. But even in their super sizes, Gertel's challahs are light and delicate. Take home a six-pound challah, sliced, and put it in your freezer. Toast a few slices at a time and slather them with butter or honey for heavenly breakfasts.

7

9

8

10

11. IL LABORATORIO DEL GELATO

The genius behind Il Laboratorio del Gelato is Jon Snyder, a man with a passion for ice cream and a flair for marketing. As a teenager, Snyder worked in his family's Carvel business, and then went on to create Ciao Bella Gelato, a boutique brand he later sold. After a short stint in banking, Jon started Il Laboratorio, an experimental ice-cream "lab," to try out new flavors and consistencies. As scientific as this may sound, the gelato here is clearly the work of artistans—dense, creamy, and delicious. Part of the credit goes to the machinery, which creates ice cream with a marvelously rich consistency. The "laboratory" brings in fresh fruits and herbs from Hunts Point and Union Square Greenmarket to create an unusual range of flavors—black sesame, rice, ginger, hazelnut, rose petal, tarragon with pink pepper, licorice, black Mission fig, mascarpone, chocolate Kahlúa, champagne, black currant, and lychee. Snyder still keeps his hand in every part of the business, from store design to logo to spoons. He grinds the almonds and hazelnuts himself to get exactly the right texture. The intense "research and development" of Il Laboratorio shows in every spoonful; this is some of the finest ice cream you will taste anywhere in the world.

BLACK MISSION FIG GELATO

IL LABORATORIO DEL GELATO /
MAKES 2 TO 3 PINTS

Making your own gelato is a lot less daunting than it sounds, and the results are amazing. You just need a home ice-cream machine and the will to make it happen. There's nothing more satisfying than telling your guests, ever so modestly, that not only did you cook dinner, but you also made the ice cream in your own laborotorio del gelato.

2 cups half-and-half

1 cup heavy cream

1 cup sugar

2 tablespoons peach preserves

1 pint fresh black Mission figs (whole or peeled)

1   In a heavy pot, combine the half-and-half, cream, sugar, and preserves and bring to a simmer over medium heat.

2   Cook for around 10 minutes, stirring occasionally.

3   Pour through a sieve into a bowl, let cool, and chill in the refrigerator overnight.

4   Crush the figs by hand and add them to the cream mixture.

5   Pour into an ice-cream machine and freeze according to the manufacturer's directions.

BITTER CHOCOLATE GELATO

IL LABORATORIO DEL GELATO /
MAKES 2 TO 3 PINTS

This is the recipe for Il Laboratorio del Gelato's best-selling flavor. Make sure the cocoa powder is at least 70 percent cacao.

1¼ cups sugar

2½ cups milk

1 cup cocoa powder

4 ounces bittersweet chocolate

5 large egg yolks

1 In a heavy saucepan, cook ¼ cup of the sugar with 1 teaspoon water over medium heat until it starts to melt. Stir until the sugar is melted and a deep brown color.

2 Remove from the heat and set the pan in a larger pan of ice water to stop the cooking. Let cool.

3 Add the milk to the pan and cook over medium heat, stirring, until the caramel is melted. Whisk in the cocoa powder and set aside.

4 In a double boiler, melt the chocolate, then set aside.

5 Beat the egg yolks together with the remaining sugar until thick and pale yellow. Gradually whisk in the milk mixture and stir in the melted chocolate.

6 Place over low heat and cook for 5 minutes.

7 Pour through a sieve into a bowl, let cool, then chill overnight.

8 Pour the mixture into an ice-cream maker and freeze according to the manufacturer's instructions.

12. THE SWEET LIFE

The Sweet Life is not just a candy store or a nut store or a dried fruit store or a chocolate store. The Sweet Life is a delightful hodgepodge of sweet and salty crammed into a space not much bigger than a Mini-Cooper. The jars of nostalgic candies—nonpareils, shoestring licorice, and Jordan almonds—sit beside displays of exquisite German honeys and syrups. Indian cashews the size of quarters are parked next to macadamias fresh off the plane from Hawaii. A massive block of halvah is ready for slicing. The selection of dried fruit is unmatched: dried apricots, peaches, pears, raisins, plums, cherries, and apples. You can buy them by the quarter pound or half ton and have them shipped anywhere in the world. You can also design your own trail mix. Then there's the chocolate: hand-dipped chocolate pretzels, chocolate marshmallows on a stick covered with M&M's, and chocolate-coated raisins, peanuts, macadamias, and almonds. At 63 Hester Street, life *is* sweet.

CRYSTALLIZED GINGER COOKIES

SWEET LIFE / MAKES ABOUT 30 COOKIES

Crystallized ginger from Sweet Life gives these cookies a light bite and rich gingery taste. You can make the dough in advance and freeze; just take it out of the freezer an hour before baking. These cookies are perfect with tea or espresso.

1 cup (2 sticks) unsalted butter, at room temperature

1 cup sugar

2¼ cups all-purpose flour

2 large eggs

5 ounces crystallized ginger

Pinch of salt

1 With an electric mixer at medium speed, beat the butter and sugar until creamy, then add the flour and the eggs.

2 Mix until the dough holds together, and add the ginger and salt.

3 Press the dough with your hands to make a roll 2 inches in diameter, and wrap it in plastic.

4 Refrigerate for 1 hour.

5 Preheat the oven to 400 degrees.

6 On a floured surface, cut the roll into ¼-inch-thick rounds and place them 2 inches apart on a nonstick cookie sheet.

7 Bake for about 10 minutes, until the edges are lightly brown. Let cool on wire racks.

CHAPTER 7

MIDTOWN

Midtown is the commercial heart of the city, twenty square blocks packed with skyscraping corporate headquarters and flagship stores displaying the world's most famous fashion brands. Midtown is home to the New York Public Library, the Museum of Modern Art, the Empire State Building, Radio City Music Hall, and the Broadway theater district. The streets here buzz with energy, day and night. Midtown also houses some of the most prestigious restaurants and food stores in Manhattan. Taking a cue from the world of fashion, many of the leading food brands have opened flagship stores in Midtown. But as you head farther west or south you'll find smaller, less established food stores every bit as interesting as their more corporate neighbors. In between 40th and 59th Streets west of Eighth Avenue, there's the newly gentrified Hell's Kitchen, which was once the turf of the toughest gangs in New York. Now the neighborhood has been renamed Clinton. Its side streets are home to an unusual mix of food shops. Another midtown enclave, Little Korea, seemed to spring up overnight. It centers on 32nd Street between Broadway and Fifth Avenue. The block is dense with Korean restaurants, karaoke bars, unidentified haunts, and of course some amazing food stores. Little Korea booms at night as many places stay open late. It's worth visiting just to see all the lights alone. So, in between dressing rooms at Barney's, Gucci, and Saks, or after a Broadway matinee, check out some of the amazing food stores to be found in the area.

1. PETROSSIAN

In one of the great ironies of the Russian Revolution, it was the spartan Bolsheviks who introduced the pleasures of caviar to the decadent French. Leon Trotsky, at the head of the Red Army, drove thousands of upper-class Russians across the border and eventually into France. These émigrés—"White Russians"—brought along their taste for smoked salmon, sturgeon, and sturgeon eggs, also known as caviar. In the 1920s Paris fell under the spell of these new émigrés. Diaghilev choreographed dances to the scores of Stravinsky, Chekhov was performed by the Comédie Française, and Raskolnikov became a cult hero. To this heady cultural whirl, the Petrossian brothers supplied the caviar. Over the decades, their little caviar store on Paris's Avenue Motte-Piquet grew into the largest importer and processor of caviar in the world. Luckily, the Petrossian family is still importing and selling caviar today. The New York store, run by Alexander Petrossian, great-grandson of the founder, offers some of the world's finest osetra, beluga, and sevruga caviar. Petrossian also sells smoked and cured salmon and herring, smoked back in Paris. The blini, waffles, and French pastries, all baked on the premises, are excellent, as are the chocolates, which are packaged in the same distinctive blue boxes as the caviar. The shopping is pricey, but you can be absolutely sure of the quality.

WARM BORSCHT SOUP

PETROSSIAN / SERVES 8

If caviar is the spirit, then borscht is the lifeblood of Russian cuisine. It's usually served cold, but this warm version will get you cozily through a winter evening.

1½ quarts chicken stock or canned chicken broth

2 teaspoons salt

1½ pounds carrots, cut into ½-inch cubes

1½ pounds beets, roasted and cut into ½-inch cubes

1 Granny Smith apple, peeled and cut into ½-inch cubes

1½ heads savoy cabbage, shredded

1½ cups honey

1½ cups balsamic vinegar

Freshly ground black pepper to taste

1½ cups crème fraîche (optional)

1   In a soup pot over medium heat, bring the stock to a simmer.

2   Add the salt and carrots and continue to simmer for 5 minutes.

3   Add the beets, apple, and cabbage and continue to simmer for another 3 minutes.

4   Add the honey, vinegar, and pepper. Stir and simmer for another 3 minutes.

5   Remove from the heat and serve with a dollop of crème fraîche. This soup can be made and stored in the refrigerator for up to 4 days.

2. RICHART

Richart, founded in Paris in the 1920s, is one of the very first modern chocolate boutiques. From the beginning, Richart startled the conventional confectionary world with its spare white stores and art-embossed chocolates. The tradition continues today in New York, where nothing distracts you from the excellent chocolates. The bestsellers are the ballotins, small collections embossed with children's drawings. We also were attracted to the collections organized around seasonal flavors like balsam or citrus. The boxes can be personalized with a printed message. Also not to be missed is the pâte de noisette, Richart's rich, creamy, entirely addictive chocolate-and-hazelnut spread.

3. MINAMOTO KITCHOAN

At this pristine Japanese shop, the craft of baking is an art form. A Zen-like calm pervades the minimalist space, underscored by Japanese music playing softly. The miniature cakes, exquisitely decorated, reside under glass. That so much artistry is devoted to these confections, each likely to disappear in one bite, speaks to the devotion of the bakers here. The shapes, names, and ingredients take some time to learn, but the shopkeepers go out of their way to help you understand the offerings, all traditional Japanese pastries made from a base of rice flour, bean-jam, and sugar. Some of our favorites are uguisumochi, sweet red beans wrapped in rice cake and a green pea flour coating, and mamedaifuku, sweet red beans wrapped in rice cake with red peas. There's also a tasty marzipan made with bean paste instead of almonds. A screen on the right side of the shop changes according to the season, and the flavors here also change, featuring seasonal fruits and nuts. In spring, try the cherry blossom flavor; in summer, the Japanese fruit gelatin and sorbets. In fall, we tried the chestnut and, in winter, the unusual and delicious cakes made with sweet potatoes.

4. CRUSH WINE & SPIRITS

Crush was created by a couple of real estate developers in partnership with Drew Nieporent, the founder of such trendy downtown eateries as Nobu, Montrachet, and Tribeca Grill. The Crush proposition is simple: Offer the best wines at the best price in a setting that enhances the wine experience. Crush is sleek, with sweeping racks of curved wood lining the walls and an elegant paneled tasting room. At the back of the store is "the Cube," an enormous, temperature-controlled room for "auction-quality" wine. The selection here is extensive and deep. Not only will you find the vineyard you're looking for; more than likely you'll find the year and the exact appellation. In addition to a staff that knows wine, Crush offers daily tastings and courses in wine appreciation.

5. POSEIDON BAKERY

Once upon a time, Greek bakeries, restaurants, and groceries lined this stretch of Ninth Avenue. Today, Poseidon Bakery, founded in 1923 by Demetrios Anagnostou, is the sole survivor. This authentic Greek pastry shop—with its blue-and-white facade and neon lights—is run by the same family and still sells its pastries straight from the tin molds in which they were baked. Don't miss the spinach and feta spanakopita, a Greek-style empanada, or the kreatopita, a meat pie, both fillings wrapped in crisp phyllo dough. You can also purchase first-rate fresh phyllo dough here for your homemade hors d'oeuvres. Kourambiedes, the Greek cookies traditionally baked for the New Year, are available here all year-round. The butter cookies, made with crushed almonds and rolled in powdered sugar, are wonderful with espresso.

さくらんぼ

寿

3

3

3

6. AMY'S BREAD

After studying at the Culinary Institute and Bouley Bakery, Amy Schreiber went to France and learned the art of baking bread from the masters. But when she opened her first bakery in Hell's Kitchen fourteen years ago, the reputation of the neighborhood was such that people told her she'd be better off opening a shop in the Balkans. But Schreiber is a courageous woman, and her store is now the cornerstone of the Hell's Kitchen renaissance. Amy's Bread is also a thriving wholesale business, but Schreiber has held on to her original vision: to offer New Yorkers world-class fresh-baked bread. Recently Amy's started making pastry, and, not surprisingly, these are excellent too. But if you have room for only one of Amy's items in your shopping basket, try the Pumpkin Walnut Cranberry Quickbread.

PUMPKIN WALNUT CRANBERRY QUICKBREAD

AMY'S BREAD /

MAKES 3 (9-BY-5-INCH) LOAVES

This recipe is one of Amy Schreiber's favorites. What makes quickbread quick is the fast-acting baking soda used for leavening in place of yeast. The bread rises as soon as liquid is added, and the delicious result is closer in texture to a scone than to bread. The autumnal mix of ingredients make this quickbread recipe from Amy's perfect for Thanksgiving.

2 cups (4 sticks) unsalted butter

8 large eggs

3¾ cups granulated sugar

4 cups cooked pureed pumpkin

6½ cups all-purpose flour

1 tablespoon plus 2 teaspoons kosher salt

1 tablespoon plus 1 teaspoon baking soda

2 teaspoons cinnamon

2 teaspoons freshly grated nutmeg

Zest of 1 large orange

3 cups combination of fresh cranberries and walnuts

¼ cup turbinado sugar

1 Preheat the oven to 350 degrees.

2 Using 2 tablespoons of the butter, grease three 9-by-5-inch loaf pans.

3 Melt the remaining butter and cool slightly.

4 Combine it with the eggs. Whisk in the granulated sugar and the pumpkin, then add 1¼ cups water.

5 In a separate bowl, combine the flour, salt, baking soda, cinnamon, nutmeg, and orange zest.

6 Pour the pumpkin mixture into the dry ingredients and fold gently until almost combined, then fold in the cranberries and nuts. Finish with a few gentle strokes to combine without overmixing.

7 Divide the batter evenly among the greased pans. Sprinkle the top of each loaf with turbinado sugar.

8 Bake for 55 to 65 minutes, until a toothpick inserted into the center comes out clean.

9 Let cool in the pans for 15 minutes, then turn the loaves out of the pans and let them cool on a wire rack. The quickbreads will keep, wrapped in plastic and refrigerated, for 2 to 3 days.

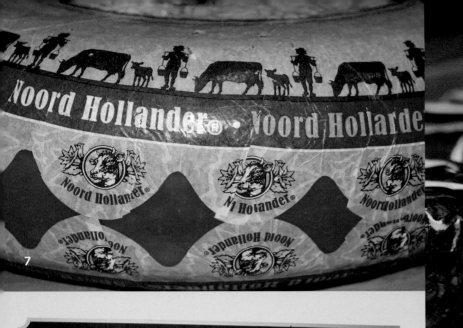

Noord Hollander® · Noord Hollander
Noord Hollander® · Ni Hollander® · Noordollander®

7

FROMAGERIE

LE CLUB FROMAGE

RETAIL   GIFT BASKETS

BERTHAUT - 21460 EPOISSES
FRANZ · WEICHKÄSE · Fabriqué par s.a. Fromagerie BERTHAUT

ISSES
d'origine
HAUT
Affiné au marc de Bourgogne
50g   A consommer de préférence
avant le : voir au dos
21.247.01
C E E
FAT IN DRY MATTER · PRODUCT OF FRANCE

EPOIS
Appellation d'
BERTHA
Fromage au lait entier aff
50 pour cent
de matière grasse   25
NET WEIGHT 9 oz · 50 % Fett i. Tr.
d'Origin

7

7

7

7. ARTISANAL

Picholine was the first American restaurant with its own temperature-controlled cheese cave. When Picholine's master fromageur, Max MacCalman, joined the midtown bistro Artisanal, he took his concept one step further. He added a cheese cave and on-site cheese shop. All of the cheeses here are truly artisanal, made by small farmers rather than large manufacturers. Max, whom you're likely to find behind the counter, has written several books on cheese and cheese-and-wine pairings. He will bring his passion to your shopping experience, guiding you through the miraculous world of cheese. Artisanal also offers classes in "cheese education." But Max gave us a few tips gratis: Never serve cheese directly from the refrigerator. Let it reach room temperature. And, in spite of what the Department of Health may say, some of the very best cheese comes from unpasteurized milk—but you'll have to go to Europe to sample those. In the meantime, head to Artisanal for the best cheeses this side of the Atlantic.

ARTISANAL BLEND FONDUE

ARTISANAL / SERVES 3 OR 4

Enameled fondue pots, vintage 1978, are yard-sale staples, and fondue—after a brief comeback—we're afraid has unjustly been relegated again to the kitchen kitsch corner. We hope this recipe, using cheese from Artisanal, will help restore the reputation of this much-maligned Swiss dish. Serve with peeled and sliced apples, vegetable crudités, or air-dried beef.

1 clove garlic, peeled

½ cup white wine

2 ounces freshly grated Comte or Beaufort cheese

2 ounces freshly grated Emmentaler cheese

2 ounces freshly grated Vacherin Fribourgeois cheese

1 tablespoon plus 1 teaspoon cornstarch

1 teaspoon fresh lemon juice

Pinch of salt

Pinch of crushed white pepper

1   Rub the inside of a fondue pot with the garlic. Place the pot over a medium-high flame and pour in the wine.

2   Bring the wine to a boil, then add the cheeses and cornstarch.

3   Stir the fondue with a wire whisk; the cheese should melt and get thick and bubbly.

4   Add the juice, salt, and pepper. Serve hot.

8. BURGUNDY WINE

Bordeaux is easy. Burgundy is hard. Burgundy Wine is an entire store dedicated to the greatness of the big Pinot Noirs. While Bordeaux proceeds in orderly fashion, from St. Émilion to Pomerol, vintage to vintage and château to château, the wines of Burgundy are ever-so-slightly organized chaos. The nomenclature is convoluted, a hodgepodge of regions, towns, hillsides, and terroirs. Sometimes just a couple of hectares make a big difference, which makes mastering the wines of Burgundy a challenge. In most wine stores, your questions about Burgundy will usually get a less-than-informed answer. At Burgundy Wine the mission is to make these great wines accessible to a wider audience. This is the place to learn about Côte de Nuit, Côte de Beaune, Volney, Gevrey Chambertin, Chambolle Musigny, La Tache, or Puligny Montrachet. Bottles are neatly arranged by region, and the staff will take the time to pick wines that match your meal. If you wander to the back of the store you'll hear the wine brokers advising customers over the phone. The store's Web site is also outstanding. Wine aficionados who already know and love Burgundy will find the selection of varieties and vintages impressive. Burgundy recently has added the Pinot Noirs of Oregon to their list as well as Côtes du Rhône.

BRAISED ASPARAGUS WITH MORELS IN CREAM
BURGUNDY WINE / SERVES 2 OR 3

We've all heard that asparagus is difficult to pair with wine, but the French, for whom the opening day of asparagus season might as well be a national holiday, have it all figured out. These wines work especially well with asparagus: Chablis, Puligny Montrachet, Savigny les Beaune, Chambolle-Musigny, Volnay, all Burgundies, and all available at Burgundy Wine.

3 shallots, chopped

3 tablespoons unsalted butter

3 ounces dried morel mushrooms, soaked overnight in a mixture of water and 1 cup white Burgundy, drained

1 cup heavy cream

Salt and freshly ground black pepper

1 pound asparagus, trimmed and peeled

1   In a large pan, sauté the shallots in 1 tablespoon of the butter until soft and beginning to brown. Add the mushrooms. Lower the heat and simmer for 10 minutes.

2   Add the cream and cook until thickened, then add salt and pepper to taste.

3   In a large sauté pan, melt the remaining butter with ½ cup water. Add the asparagus and salt and pepper to taste. Cook over medium heat, covered, for 2 minutes.

4   Uncover and cook over high heat, shaking the pan, until the water has evaporated and the asparagus is glazed with butter. Pour the cream and mushroom sauce over the asparagus and serve.

9. GRAND CENTRAL MARKET

Grand Central Market, located in Grand Central Terminal, has a potential customer base of about 200,000 daily commuters from Westchester, Putnam County, and Connecticut. From the bustling activity in the market, it's likely that a large percentage are bringing *filets de dorade* back to Darien and Westphalian ham back to suburban Rye. Shopping for dinner at this glorious market before catching the train is a complete pleasure. The fish store, Pescatore, offers a full array of fresh seafood. Greenwich Produce displays a vast selection of fresh fruits and vegetables. You'll also find branches of Murray's Cheese, Ceriello, the Italian butcher and specialty shop, and Koglin German Hams. This is Koglin's only American store (with four in Germany), and the charcuterie here is superb. If you've spent a tough day at the office—any office—and you're ready to retreat to Greenwich or even Greenwich Village, buy your family dinner here and avoid that second commute to the local supermarket.

SALMON AND CHANTERELLES

The salmon at Pescatore is as fresh as it comes, and that's what's required for this unusual combination of powerful ingredients. Surprisingly, the chanterelles and salmon come together to create a wonderful new taste that is neither fish nor fungus. Garnish the dish with simply cooked seasonal vegetables..

FOR THE FISH STOCK

4 pounds trimmings, bones, heads of white-fleshed, nonoily fish (no guts, no gills)

2 large onions, unpeeled, cut into large chunks

2 heads garlic, cut in half horizontally

2 cups dry white wine

FOR THE SALMON

1 pound chanterelles

4 tablespoons unsalted butter

4 (6-ounce) salmon fillets

2 cups dry white wine

1 tablespoon finely chopped shallot

Juice of ½ lemon

½ teaspoon Dijon mustard

¼ cup heavy cream

1 tablespoon chopped fresh chervil

MAKE THE FISH STOCK

1   Rinse the fish bones. Combine all four ingredients in a large stockpot with 4 quarts cold water. The liquid should cover the solids by 4 inches.

2   Bring to a boil, skim the foam from the top, then reduce the heat and simmer for 25 to 30 minutes.

3   Strain through a fine-mesh sieve, let cool to room temperature, cover, and store in the refrigerator. The stock will keep for 4 to 5 days, or in the freezer for up to 6 months.

MAKE THE SALMON

1   Carefully clean the mushrooms with a pastry brush or paper towels and sauté them in a frying pan with the butter over medium-high heat, until the mushrooms release their liquid, approximately 10 minutes. Chanterelles give off a lot of moisture when cooked.

2   Remove from the heat and set aside, reserving the liquid.

3   Place the salmon fillets in a saucepan with a tight-fitting lid. Add the wine and enough of the fish stock to come about halfway up the salmon. Add the shallots and the mushroom liquid.

4   Cover tightly and cook over medium heat for 3 to 4 minutes, until the fish is lightly cooked.

5   Remove the fish from the liquid and set aside; keep warm.

6   Add the mushrooms and cook over high heat to reduce the liquid by half.

7   Add the lemon juice, mustard, and cream. Bring to a boil and cook to reduce until very slightly thickened. Season to taste with salt and additional lemon if necessary. Add the chervil.

8   Place the salmon on warm serving plates. Pour the sauce and mushrooms over the salmon.

10. VINO

Vino sells only Italian wines. Even if you've only dabbled at Chianti, by the time you've sampled some of the vintages here you may decide to devote a lifetime to learning and loving the wines of Italy. Every wine-producing region of Italy is represented at Vino. From Tuscany: Brunello, Carmignano, San Gimignano, Montepulciano, and some incredible super-Tuscans. From Piedmont: Barbaresco, Barolo, Dolcetta, Barbera. Add to these the wines of Puglia, Sicily, Sardinia, Umbria, Abruzzo, Valle d'Aosta, and Veneto. At Vino you will be delighted by the depth as well as the breadth of the selection. You will find here more producers and more good vintages of any one variety than you can find just about anywhere outside of Italy. On our first visit we followed the staff's enthusiastic recommendation and selected a 1989 Barbaresco that was spectacular. That's the other great thing about Vino: The staff takes the time to explain and to let you taste. Before you order a case they will insist that you try a bottle.

11. SPICE CORNER

Spice Corner holds the distinction of being the purveyor of spices to the United Nations neighborhood since 1950. Chances are that the owners of this family-run spice shop remember the name of every diplomat who has crossed their threshold. It used to be that shopping for Indian products was nearly impossible without speaking the languages of the subcontinent. But the gentlemen staffing the Spice Corner are so helpful that you're sure to walk out with products you never imagined buying. You will learn all the uses for the betel leaf, dry curry leaves, and sumac. You will find out which ayurvedic medicine treats each and every one of your ailments. You will be encouraged to sample the spices, jams, and prepared dishes. We especially recommend the babam bashi, a sweet pastry made from crushed almonds.

12. INTERNATIONAL GROCERY

The facade of this Ninth Avenue grocery is unprepossessing, but as soon as you walk in you are steeped in the ambience of an Istanbul souk. Workers sit on bags of spices, eating soup and waiting for customers. Dino, the owner, who would not reveal his last name, is truly an international man of mystery. Dino presides with the breezy charm of a Middle Eastern trader and loves to tell stories that may be true or fabulist tales—it doesn't matter. The spices here, sold by the pound, are very fresh. The selection of flours is extensive—soy, high gluten, buckwheat, chickpea, and potato. Walk over to Ninth Avenue and stop into International. Chat with Dino and listen to his tales (the grain of salt is at hand), and stock up on the wonderful spices and flours offered here.

13. HAN AH REUM

Han Ah Reum could be Korean for "hard to find." All the signage leading to this remarkable grocery is in Korean; once you arrive, you might mistake this place for an adult video shop. However, once inside, it's all groceries. One of the unique wonders of Han Ah Reum is the amazing selection of thinly sliced meats and fish for Korean-style barbecue—sirloin, pork shoulder, strip steak, striped bass, yellowtail. The slices are already marinated and ready for the grill. The Korean snacks are unusual and intriguing—stir-fried anchovies, salted codfish, heavily seasoned dried spinach. In the vegetable section you'll find a plentiful selection of mushrooms and fresh sesame leaves, wonderful for wrapping fish on the grill. You will also find several varieties of kimchi, the traditional Korean sauce made from fermented vegetables and soy sauce. Han Ah Reum is the biggest and best Korean supermarket in New York, a great place to make new discoveries. All you have to do is find the place.

14. KALUSTYAN'S

If spice was still used as currency, Kalustyan's could be the Federal Reserve. Founded in 1944, Kalustyan's is the largest retail spice dealer in New York City. They supply most of the great restaurants, but they will gladly sell you a few ounces or a few hundred pounds of any spice on your list. Kalustyan's new owners have expanded the store's products so that, alongside Asian and Indian spices, you will find arborio rice from Italy, green lentils from France, and olive oil from Greece. In fact, the store carries 190 different types of rice and 96 different varieties of lentils and dals. You will also find salt from the Himalayas, chutneys from southern India, and pistachios from Iran. Kalustyan's full list of products can be found on its Web site, but don't pass up a visit to this remarkable store, one of those magical places in New York where you can shop with your nose.

CORN PAKORAS
KALUSTYAN'S / SERVES 4

We used ingredients from Kalustyan's to make these pakoras. They make great hors d'oeuvres or can be served as an accompaniment to a curry dinner.

1 cup all-purpose flour

1 teaspoon baking powder

½ teaspoon salt

½ teaspoon chili powder

½ cup milk

1 cup sweet corn

½ teaspoon garlic pulp

2 fresh red chiles, seeded and minced

1 medium onion, finely diced

1 large egg

1 cup finely chopped scallions

1 cup corn oil

1 Mix all the ingredients except the oil together to form a batter.

2 Heat the oil in a deep frying pan.

3 Drop spoonfuls of the batter into the oil about 5 at a time. When lightly browned, turn them over and brown the other side, about 5 to 10 minutes total.

4 Remove with a slotted spoon and drain on paper towels. Serve with sweet chile sauce for dipping.

CHAPTER 8

SOHO

Soho, the neighborhood south of Houston Street, spreads south to Canal Street and east from Hudson Street to Lafayette Street. For us, the neighborhood divides into two distinct parts, each with its own feel and character. You won't find our subtle subdivision on any map, but we call the two areas Soho Major and Soho Minor.

The area we call Soho Major began as a nameless neighborhood of factories and warehouses lodged in beautifully proportioned nineteenth-century cast-iron buildings. Later in the late sixties and early seventies, swarms of young artists were lured to Soho by low rents and turned the huge factory loft spaces into illegal live-in studios. Through the eighties and nineties fashion followed art, and the bare lofts, now legitimized, became magnificent homes for the trendy and famous. At store level, funky plumbing supply companies, old-world family fabric businesses, and suppliers of leather goods for the shoe trade gave way to some of the world's most luxurious boutiques and

restaurants. Rem Koolhaas designed Prada's new flagship store at the corner of Broadway and Prince. Magnates of media, fashion, and finance now pay millions to live in what used to be shoe factories.

Soho Minor lives in the spaces between the grand buildings and on blocks of tenements that have not yet been gilded by the developer's touch. The scale here is smaller, the feeling more intimate. Tomorrow's writers, painters, designers, musicians, filmmakers, and technocrats work and live side by side with old-timers whose families settled the neighborhood in the late nineteenth century.

But, for us, in either area it's the food stores that make Soho exciting—they're as authentic as the architecture and as diverse as the Sunday crowds. No matter where you are in Soho, you're always just a few steps from some of New York's most remarkable food stores.

1. JOE'S DAIRY

Near the corner of Sullivan and Houston is an unremarkable storefront that would be easy to hurry past a thousand times and never notice. But walk by Joe's Dairy just once, and you will be frozen in your tracks, stopped by the wonderfully enticing aroma of *latticini freschi*—the mozzarella made fresh every day inside. The seductive scent only hints at the delectable marvels in store. There's one mozzarella for pizza, another for sandwiches, and another for fresh tomatoes; mozzarella made from whole milk, skim milk, or buffalo milk; smoked mozzarella, salted mozzarella, and unsalted mozzarella. The process may be simple, but the difference between a tasteless lump of white cheese and a magnificent mozzarella is all in the touch of the cheese maker, and at Joe's the touch is as delicate and refined as any this side of Naples.

2. PINO MEATS

Directly across Sullivan Street from Joe's, is another old-school, old-world gem, Pino Meats. The maestro here is Pino Cinquemani who started Pino's fifty years ago and still works behind the counter every day. There were five generations of Cinquemani butchers before Pino, and when he came to New York from Sicily he brought with him the family obsession: a passion for the perfect cut. Pino believes that giving his customers the finest beef, pork, and poultry—which he always does—is only the beginning. The real art is in the cutting, and here Pino is without peer. His steaks, chops, and roasts are perfectly proportioned, with just the right amount of fat and bone. A Pino's New York strip cooked medium-rare is sirloin satori. The Thanksgiving turkeys here are legend, and every November pilgrims from up and down the East Coast trek to Pino's for their holiday bird.

3. GRANDAISY BAKERY

Behind the tiny retail space at the front of the store is a huge bakery, a floury wonderland where the bakers make their crusty breads fresh every morning. The pizzas here are unique—six feet long and four inches wide, baked on long wooden boards, and then cut into crunchy rectangular slices. There's pizza bianca with olive oil, rosemary, and salt or the schiatta d'uva with champagne grapes, raisins, and fennel seed. Their just-baked panettone, fresh out of the oven, is as light and airy as a Christmas carol.

4. DEAN & DELUCA

Dean & DeLuca, which started in the late seventies as Giorgio DeLuca's tiny cheese store on Prince Street, has grown into a high-end theme park for food lovers in a landmark building on Broadway. White-coated salespeople preside over this soaring, white-columned, marble-floored expanse dedicated to the proposition that when it comes to food, more is better: more choice, more variety, and more quality. On shimmering stainless steel racks, in glistening glass cases, in barrels and urns, in tureens, and on trays you'll find the finest meats, fish, chocolate, pastry, caviar, sturgeon, charcuterie, truffles, prepared food, candies, cakes, syrups, jams, and bread. Shopping for mustard? You'll find varieties from France, England, Sweden, and Germany. Buying olives here is a geography lesson: kalamata, gaeta, Basque, lucque, Catalan, Casablanca mixed, Provençal, cigniopia, castelvetrano, picholine. With sixty different oils (thirty of which are olive) and thirty-seven different varieties of vinegar, the possibilities for salad dressing alone are infinite. At Dean & DeLuca the selection is so vast, there's a good chance you'll find imported brands that are unavailable in the country they came from.

5. RAVIOLI STORE

The Ravioli Store was founded by Michael Nasoff, a former advertising executive who woke up one morning and decided he had to buy the old pasta store down the block and make ravioli his life's work. In New York this sort of conversion happens every day. Lawyers become chefs, bankers become bakers, and doctors become pâtissiers. So, in 1989, Nasoff bought out the previous owners and began making fresh ravioli and pasta from scratch every day of the week. Nasoff is to ravioli what Giotto was to the fresco. The art is in the fillings: aged goat cheese with herbs in a peppercorn pasta, wild mushrooms with truffles in saffron pasta, lobster, lump crab, and forty-eight more flavorful Italian dumplings. You can find Nasoff and his crew hard at work every morning—when you are obsessed there are no holidays—slicing enormous wheels of goat cheese, mixing fillings, and cutting squares of pasta. If the Met ever does a ravioli retrospective you can be sure Nasoff's work will be front and center.

BUTTERNUT SQUASH RAVIOLI IN SAGE BUTTER
RAVIOLI STORE /
6 SERVINGS (MAKES 18 RAVIOLI)

Michael Nasoff of the Ravioli Store has devoted his life to ravioli, but you can make his favorite in an afternoon. You can assemble and cut the ravioli up to a day in advance (don't boil them): Sprinkle them lightly with cornmeal to prevent sticking and store them, covered, in the refrigerator.

FOR FILLING

4 pounds butternut squash (about 3 medium-sized squash)

2 tablespoons olive oil

Salt and pepper, to taste

6 tablespoons (¾ stick) unsalted butter, divided

2 bay leaves

¼ teaspoon cayenne pepper

1 tablespoon cinnamon

¼ teaspoon ground cloves

¼ teaspoon freshly grated nutmeg

¼ teaspoon freshly ground white pepper

¼ teaspoon lightly crumbled saffron

1 teaspoon salt

20 amaretti cookies

1 cup freshly grated Pecorino Romano

FOR FRESH PASTA

2 cups semolina flour

2 large eggs, lightly beaten

3 tablespoons finely chopped fresh sage, plus extra whole leaves for garnish

TO MAKE THE FILLING

1   Preheat the oven to 400 degrees.

2   Halve each squash and scoop out seeds. Drizzle each cut half with olive oil and season with salt and freshly ground black pepper. Roast, cut side down, 40 to 60 minutes, until the squash is cooked through and tender.

3   After the roasted squash is cool enough to touch, scoop out the meat and mash with a fork.

4   Melt 2 tablespoons of the butter in a sauté pan over medium heat. Add the bay leaves, cayenne pepper, cinnamon, cloves, nutmeg, white pepper, saffron, and salt. Cook on a low flame until the butter browns slightly, about 5 minutes. Be careful not to burn the butter.

5   Pulse the cookies in a food processor until finely ground. You should have about ½ cup of crumbs.

6   Add the cookie crumbs and cheese to the squash and mix well.

7   Remove the bay leaves from the spice-butter mixture and stir into the squash.

8   Let the filling rest at room temperature while you make the pasta.

TO MAKE THE PASTA

1   Put the flour in a large, deep bowl and shape a well in the center. Pour the beaten eggs into the well, and gradually mix the flour into the eggs with a fork.

2   Place the dough on a floured work surface. If the dough is sticky, sprinkle it with flour. Gently knead the dough until it forms a smooth, elastic ball, about 10 minutes. Dust the dough with flour, wrap it in plastic, and refrigerate for 30 minutes.

3   Roll the dough into two long sheets, each about 24 inches long, 12 inches wide, and ⅛ inch thick.

TO MAKE THE RAVIOLI

1   Lay one sheet of pasta on a lightly floured work surface.

2   Space rounded tablespoonfuls of filling on the pasta four inches apart, in three rows of six. Lightly brush around each mound of filling with water, and lay the remaining sheet of pasta on top. Lightly press around each mound of filling to create a seal. Using a sharp knife or pastry wheel, cut out the 18 individual ravioli.

3   Bring a large pot of salted water to a boil and cook the ravioli until al dente, about 5 minutes.

4   As the ravioli cooks, melt the remaining 4 tablespoons of butter in a small saucepan. When the butter stops foaming, add the chopped sage and cook until lightly crispy.

5   Arrange the cooked and drained ravioli on a platter and drizzle with the sage-butter sauce. Garnish with small whole sage leaves and serve.

6

7

7

6. KEE'S CHOCOLATES

When you turn the corner onto Thompson Street, the powerful aroma of chocolate wafting from Kee's Chocolates conjures visions of Willy Wonka's immense factory. But Kee Ling Tong's tiny shop on Thompson is about the size of a box of Milk Duds, though the chocolate she turns out is extraordinary. Kee Ling Tong is the mad genius here behind everything: She creates the recipes, mixes the chocolate, makes the molds, stocks the displays, and serves the customers. This artisan's unique touch is what makes the chocolates at Kee's so remarkable.

7. THE YOGHURT PLACE II

Immediately next door to Grandaisy Bakery is The Yoghurt Place II. This is yogurt made the Greek way. In the small villages of Greece women make yogurt in a large ceramic jar, mixing a dollop of the family's secret yogurt culture—every family has one—with fresh milk, then leaving it on the windowsill to warm slowly in the Aegean sun. The gentle heat helps the culture grow, and eventually the mixture takes on a thick and creamy texture. This yogurt is a classic Greek breakfast, served on toasted bread with garlic and olive oil. There is no other yogurt in the world this good. The Yoghurt Place II doesn't exactly use a windowsill—they have a modern facility in Queens—but they still make their yogurt the slow, natural, Greek way. And while you're in the store, be sure to strike up a conversation with Vea Kessioglou, the owner and proprietor. Her genuine warmth and caring is part of what makes exploring small stores and kitchens such as these so rewarding.

TZATZIKI
THE YOGHURT PLACE II / SERVES 4

Tzatziki is a refreshing classic Greek condiment that's great as a dip with pita bread or as a sauce for grilled or roasted meats and vegetables. Make a big batch—you'll be surprised how quickly tzatziki disappears.

1 cucumber, peeled and shredded against the coarse side of a box grater

1 pound Greek yogurt

2 tablespoons chopped fresh dill

1 clove garlic, finely chopped

1 teaspoon salt

½ teaspoon freshly ground black pepper

2 tablespoons olive oil

1 tablespoon white vinegar

1 Squeeze the shredded cucumber with your hands to drain most of the water, and pat dry with a paper towel.

2 In a large bowl, combine the cucumber with the yogurt and dill.

3 Mix the garlic, salt, pepper, olive oil, and vinegar and add it to the yogurt mixture. Stir to combine.

4 Cover and chill in the refrigerator for at least half an hour.

5 Season to taste with additional salt and pepper, and serve chilled.

8. DOM'S

Lower Lafayette toward Canal is still Soho, but somehow the tides of gentrification have so far left these few blocks relatively untouched. And here you'll find Dom's salumeria, its windows lit with ancient neon signs. Dom's is directly across from the old Police Building, and it's easy to imagine Serpico, Kojac, and Barney Miller on line together in front of the counter, waiting for one of Dom's signature sandwiches. The shelves here are stocked with pastas and sauces you will find nowhere else. The meats, cut to order at the old-fashioned butcher counter, are superb, and at lunchtime the store is packed with locals calling out numbers from a huge menu posted overhead. Each number corresponds to one of Dom's custom-tailored hero sandwiches. Try the #15—it was Popeye Doyle's favorite.

9. EILEEN'S SPECIAL CHEESECAKE

At the first Olympic games in 320 BC, the Greeks served cheesecake as a sort of PowerBar for the athletes, and ever since the world has strived for excellence in both athletics and cheesecake. There is nothing classical about the one-story building at 17 Cleveland Place that houses Eileen's Special Cheesecake, but this tiny shop is cheesecake's Mount Olympus. The universal recipe for cheesecake is simple: cream cheese, eggs, sour cream, sugar, vanilla, and lemon juice, but Eileen Avezzano has figured out exactly the right proportions to make the lightest, fluffiest cheesecake you'll ever taste. One bite of the cheesecake here will more than compensate for the decor, which hasn't been touched since the early seventies AD.

10. VESUVIO BAKERY

In 1920 Vesuvio Bakery first opened for business on Prince Street in a tenement building that is now a Soho Landmark. The stenciled tin storefront, re-painted again and again in pale green, conjures images of a New York that for the most part exists now just in memory. The store only recently changed hands and the new proprietors have gone to great lengths to preserve the traditions of this very special bakery. The breads, breadsticks, and ciabatta are made with the original recipes and baked in the same wood-burning oven. The scent of warm bread from Vesuvio wafting along Prince is as much a part of Soho experience as are the cobbled streets.

11. BALTHAZAR BAKERY

Proust had his madeleines to take him back to lost times, and denizens of Soho have their own patisserie time machine. As you enter Balthazar Bakery, breathe in the earthy smell of baking bread and pastry, then look around: You're in France, the year is 1910, and the place, a corner boulangerie. The crusty baguette here is tasty enough to pass the toughest Parisian muster. The airy brioche dissolves in the deep, dark coffee. The buttery, crisp croissants, in happy contrast to the leaden crescents New Yorkers have put up with for years, seem to float on the plate. The miche, a round, hard-crusted bread with the Balthazar "B" embossed on the side, is perfect for rough slicing into a hearty breakfast tartine. At Balthazar Bakery antique silver-leafed mirrors and old oak cases speak of the past, but the baked goods here are present perfect.

12. ONCE UPON A TART

If you walk just a little farther down Sullivan, you can't miss the always original window displays at Once Upon A Tart. Fourteen years ago, just arrived from France, Jerome Audureau realized that no one in New York knew how to make his favorite food, the savory tart. Back then New York's tart vocabulary was limited to sweet—linzer, apple, or raspberry. As a result Audureau, who learned to cook from a Raymond Oliver cookbook he found in his mother's kitchen, made it his mission to convert New York to the savory tart. And, thanks largely to his efforts, we've begun, quiche by quiche, to appreciate the savory side of tartdom. Experimenting with traditional French recipes in his New York kitchen, Audureau worked obsessively to perfect his savory tarts. And perfect they are: At Once Upon A Tart you'll find spinach-mushroom, roasted bell pepper, mushroom-potato, tomato provençal, and more—each baked in a light and flaky crust.

PROVENÇAL TART

ONCE UPON A TART /

EACH 9-INCH TART SERVES 6

If memories of past picnics conjure up visions of mayonnaise-laden salads cooking in the hot sun, then you'll appreciate this savory tart, made to keep well even on the most sweltering summer day. Wait for the height of the tomato season to make this pro- vençal favorite. The tart crusts can be prepared in advance and frozen.

FOR THE CRUST

2½ cups unbleached all-purpose flour

3 tablespoons semolina flour

1 teaspoon salt

12 tablespoons (1½ sticks) unsalted butter, chilled and cut into ¼-inch cubes

3 tablespoons solid vegetable shortening, chilled

Ceramic pie weights (available in most baking supply stores) or dried pinto beans

FOR THE TART

9-inch tart shell, as prepared above

2½ pounds plum tomatoes (about 12 to 15), cored and sliced into ¼-inch-thick rounds

2 tablespoons Dijon mustard

1 cup coarsely grated Gruyère cheese

1 teaspoon herbes de Provence

2 large eggs

¼ cup light cream

1 teaspoon salt

A few turns of freshly ground black pepper

TO MAKE THE CRUST

1 Combine the flours and salt in the bowl of a food processor fitted with a metal blade and pulse a couple of times to mix.

2 Add butter and shortening; pulse until the mixture takes on a sandy texture and no large chunks of butter or shortening remain. Do not overmix.

3 Place the dough into a big bowl and sprinkle the surface with 4 tablespoons of ice water.

4 Use your hands or a wooden spoon to shape the dough into a ball, adding more water, 1 tablespoon at a time, as needed. The dough should just hold together, remaining somewhat crumbly.

5 Halve the dough and wrap each half in plastic. With the palm of your hand, press each half to form a disk. Refrigerate at least 30 minutes before rolling out. You can freeze any unused dough well wrapped.

6 Gently roll out the dough, rolling out from the center to the edge, until it is ¼ inch thick. Fit the rolled dough into a 9-inch tart pan with a removable bottom and chill in the refrigerator for 30 minutes. Trim excess dough by running a knife along the edge of the pan. Use a fork to make small holes over the entire bottom of the tart.

7 Position oven racks so that one is in the center and preheat the oven to 400 degrees.

8 Line the dough with parchment paper or aluminum foil and weigh down with pie weights or dried beans.

9 Bake on the center rack in the oven for 10 minutes. Remove the paper or foil and weights. Return pan to the oven and bake another 10 minutes.

10 Remove the tart shell from the oven and set it on a wire rack to cool. Cover and keep at room temperature.

TO MAKE THE TART

1 Position oven racks so that one is in the center and preheat the oven to 375 degrees.

2 Put the tomato slices in a colander in the sink. Let tomatoes sit for 15 minutes to drain off any excess liquid.

3 Spread the mustard evenly over the bottom of the tart shell with a rubber spatula or the back of a spoon. Sprinkle the cheese over the mustard and the herbes de Provence over the cheese.

4 Working from the outside in, line the tart with the tomato slices, overlapping slightly in concentric circles.

5 In a small bowl, whisk the eggs just enough to break up the yolks. Mix in the cream, salt, and pepper—this is the custard. Pour the custard evenly over the tomatoes, up to about ¼ inch below the top edge of the crust. (If you don't have enough custard, add a little more cream.)

6 Bake for 1 hour to 1 hour and 20 minutes, or until the custard is set.

7 Remove the tart from the oven and set it on a wire rack to cool. Serve warm or at room temperature.

13. MARIEBELLE NEW YORK

Beauty, quality, creativity: is this the mission statement for a) The Uffizi, b) Cooper Union, or c) MarieBelle Chocolates? The answer, of course, is MarieBelle, and this sublime Soho chocolatier actually lives up to her high standard. MarieBelle's aesthetic gives the store its aura of beauty. The elegant windows are piled high with MarieBelle's signature blue and red boxes, each filled with deep brown chocolate. Inside the store, the chocolates are set like jewels in antique Italian apothecary cases, and again the blue and red theme delights the eye. The quality of MarieBelle's chocolate—up to 72 percent cacao—is as unequivocal as the taste. Saffron, cardamom, and bergamot are just a few of the surprising flavors that will push even the most jaded chocoholic's chocolate meter to the red line. Creativity is everywhere. The chocolate café tucked away at the back of the store looks like a stage set for a Hans Christian Andersen fairy tale. Here you can try MarieBelle's Aztec Hot Chocolate, made from pure Belgian cacao and sugar, along with Iced Chocolate, Chocolate Pudding, and a Hot Chocolate Toddy spiked with tequila. After a cold winter walk along cobblestone streets, MarieBelle's deep, dark chocolate makes a beautiful finish to a Soho afternoon.

13

MOLTEN CHOCOLATE CAKE

MARIEBELLE NEW YORK / SERVES 2

Accompanied by a few glasses of Beaumes de Venise, this luxurious cake makes the perfect finish to a romantic meal for two.

3½ tablespoons (about ½ stick) unsalted butter, chilled and cut into small cubes

¼ cup MarieBelle's Aztec Dark Hot Chocolate mix

1 large egg, beaten

2 tablespoons confectioners' sugar

1 tablespoon plus 1 teaspoon all-purpose flour

½ cup crème fraîche or whipped cream

1 Preheat the oven to 350 degrees. Butter two 4-inch (or 6-ounce) ramekins and set aside.

2 Melt the butter along with the chocolate mix in the top of a double boiler (or in a heatproof bowl set in a saucepan of simmering water), over medium-low heat, stirring. Set aside to cool.

3 Whisk the egg with the sugar until lumps disappear. Slowly mix the flour into the egg mixture with a wooden spoon until just combined. Stir in the cooled chocolate mixture.

4 Pour the batter into the buttered ramekins, and set the ramekins in a baking pan. Create a water bath by adding enough hot (not boiling) water to come halfway up the sides of the ramekins.

5 Bake about 15 minutes, until the tops are just set. Timing here is critical, so watch carefully—this way the center will remain perfectly molten. Let the cakes cool slightly. Serve with crème fraîche or whipped cream.

14. GOURMET GARAGE

In Soho during the early eighties it was a lot easier to find plumbing supplies, wholesale lingerie, or a No-guchi coffee table than broccoli, potatoes, and a pound of ground beef for the evening's meat loaf. As more and more families moved into the neighborhood it became clear that something very important was missing: an all-in-one food store with everyday prices and a selection of food sophisticated enough to satisfy a discerning Soho appetite. So, two neighborhood guys, Andy Arons and Adam Hartman, decided to open their own supermar-ket—and not just any supermarket, but a supermarket with a philosophy. Gourmet Garage brings Arons's idea to life. "Food is an international common denominator and I wanted to demystify gourmet food and give it everyday appeal and pricing." Everything is simply stacked, con-tributing to a warehouse feel, but you are surrounded by gourmet food from all over the world. Along one aisle, you'll find an extensive array of breads; in the next, a global selection of packaged foods. The fruits and veg-etables are flown in from six continents, and if anything grew on Antarctica, you'd probably find it here. Think of Gourmet Garage as a sort of Design Within Reach for fine food.

HERB-CRUSTED LAMB CHOPS WITH POLENTA

GOURMET GARAGE / SERVES 4

This innovative but easy recipe adds a new dimension to rack of lamb. Ask your butcher to "french" the racks—this entails trimming the fat and exposing the ends of the bones—and make sure your sauté pan can go in the oven. Panko are coarse Japanese-style bread crumbs and are widely available in most grocery stores or Asian markets.

2 racks of lamb, frenched (a single rack is 8 ribs)

Salt and freshly ground black pepper

⅓ cup chopped fresh rosemary

⅓ cup chopped fresh thyme

⅓ cup chopped fresh parsley

1½ cups panko bread crumbs

1 cup Dijon mustard

Olive oil

1 Preheat the oven to 350 degrees.

2 Season the lamb with salt and pepper to taste.

3 Combine the bread crumbs with the rosemary, thyme, and parsley in a large bowl.

4 Brush a thin layer of mustard onto the top side of the lamb and coat with the bread crumb mixture.

5 In a large, oven-safe sauté pan over a medium-high flame, heat the olive oil. Sear the herb-crusted side of lamb until golden brown. Repeat with the other side, about 15 minutes total.

6 Transfer the pan with the lamb into the preheated oven. While the lamb is in the oven, prepare the polenta (see recipe, below).

7 Roast until an instant-read thermometer inserted into the thickest part of the meat reads 127 degrees for medium-rare, about 20 minutes. Remove from the oven, and let the meat rest for a few minutes. Cut each rack so the chops are two bones thick, and serve with polenta.

POLENTA

2 cups soft chèvre (fresh goat cheese)

1 cup chopped fresh basil

2 cups whole milk

1½ teaspoons salt

1 cup polenta or yellow cornmeal

½ teaspoon freshly ground black pepper

4 tablespoons (½ stick) unsalted butter

½ cup freshly grated Parmesan cheese (about 4 ounces)

¼ cup chopped parsley

1 Combine the chèvre and basil in a medium bowl and set aside.

2 In a large pot over medium-high heat, bring the milk, 1½ cups of water, and salt to a boil.

3 Gradually mix in the polenta, whisking constantly to prevent lumps.

4 Cover and reduce the heat to low. Cook, stirring occasionally with a wooden spoon, about 20 minutes, until creamy.

5 Remove the polenta from the heat and stir in the pepper, butter, Parmesan, and parsley.

6 To serve, ladle the polenta into ramekins or small dishes, filling each about halfway. Crumble the basil-chèvre mixture on top, and finish with another dollop of polenta.

15. VINTAGE NEW YORK

If you saw a sign saying "Drink Local" in a wine shop in Burgundy or Chianti, you would think nothing of it. But seen on Broome Street, it definitely catches the eye. The increasingly uneasy wine experts of Bordeaux, Napa, and Montepulciano have always contended that the odds of New York State producing truly great wines are about as long as those on the Knicks ever winning another championship. But Vintage New York is a Soho wine store dedicated to knocking these wine snobs off their high horses. It sells and serves only wines produced in New York State—mainly from the Finger Lakes, the Hudson Valley, and Long Island. The wine bar/tasting room at Vintage New York is the perfect place to put aside prejudices and experience the subtleties of New York's finest wines.

LONG ISLAND DUCK MEATBALLS
VINTAGE NEW YORK /
SERVES 4 (ABOUT 24 MEATBALLS)

It's hard to imagine now, but the East End of Long Island was once the duck farming capital of the United States. Most of the duck farms have been replaced by elegant estates, but Long Island duck, even if it comes from the Hudson Valley, is still a flavorful treat. D'Artagnan (www.dartagnan.com) is a wonderful New York source for duck.

1½ pounds duck breast (with skin on)

⅓ cup finely chopped dried apricots

¼ cup finely chopped macadamia nuts

1 cup finely chopped Spanish onion

1 cup finely chopped celery

½ cup finely chopped leek (white part only)

½ cup finely chopped scallion

2 eggs, lightly beaten

½ cup stale bread crumbs

1 Trim all fat from the duck breast meat. Measure 3 ounces of fat; discard the remaining fat or reserve for another use. Chop the meat and reserved fat coarsely and then grind well in a food processor.

2 Combine all ingredients in a large bowl and mix well with a fork. Chill the mixture in the refrigerator for about an hour to let the flavors marry.

3 Preheat the oven to 475 degrees. Roll the chilled duck mixture into 1-inch balls, about the size of walnuts.

4 Place the meatballs on a sheet pan, leaving about 2 inches between each (so they don't steam). Roast until nicely browned, about 12 minutes.

CHAPTER 9

UNION SQUARE & CHELSEA

Here we've combined two adjoining neighborhoods: Union Square and Chelsea. Union Square encompasses a large neighborhood that begins at the Flatiron Building on Twenty-third and Broadway and radiates in a large triangle southwest and east to Fourteenth Street, bounded on the west by Sixth Avenue and on the east by Park Avenue.

In the 1930s Union Square was a nexus of the American labor movement; many unions were headquartered in the office buildings that surround the park. Later Union Square was home to Andy Warhol's Factory. These days the Union Square area is a mixed commercial and residential neighborhood housing fashion photographers, filmmakers, Internet companies, ad agencies, and loft-dwelling families.

Chelsea, west of Seventh Avenue, was once a sleepy neighborhood of graceful brownstones, old trees, and small shops. The Episcopal Seminary gives the area the character of a Cambridge college. Over the past decade, Chelsea has been discovered by artists of every generation and their dealers. The neighborhood now extends to the industrial blocks west of Tenth Avenue and encompasses a lively mix of edgy galleries, late-night clubs, and trendy restaurants. Central Chelsea retains its bucolic charm; the brownstones are still graceful, especially the elegant house where Clement Clark Moore wrote "'Twas the Night before Christmas" (marked by a bronze plaque).

Bookended by the Union Square Greenmarket to the east and Chelsea Market to the west, these two neighborhoods brim with exciting new food stores.

1. CITY BAKERY

You'll find three distinct crowds at City Bakery: local moms who bring their kids for hot chocolate and cookies; office workers grabbing a quick, tasty lunch, and Internet, film, and media moguls future, present, and past who use City Bakery as a virtual office. Although City Bakery is billed as a high-end cafeteria-style restaurant, its claim to glory rests on first-rate desserts and baked goods. Chef Ilene Rosen's chocolate tart is exquisitely sensual, maybe because one of the ingredients is a Milky Way bar. The pretzel-croissant combines sweet and salty flavors in just the right proportions and goes well with a frothy cappuccino. Children love the pillowy homemade marshmallows and oversized cookies. And don't miss out on City Bakery's signature hot chocolate—creamy and thick, hot or cold.

2. N.Y. CAKE & BAKING DISTRIBUTOR

Whatever you're planning to bake, from a tray of butter cookies to a multi-tier marzipan wedding cake, start here, at the Home Depot of baking supplies. But don't expect orderly aisles; here the displays stack silicone cookie molds next to pastry bags with interchangeable nozzles, all precariously balanced on columns of Valrhona chocolate. One wall displays edible flowers, food colorants, powdered icing, edible gold leaf, cartoon decals, and a fabulous array of cookie cutters. A serious baker might spend a few days here, browsing the awesome arsenal of baking trays, cake pans, dough cutters, electric mixers, and other plug-in gadgets. Even if you consider yourself baking-averse, this store will arouse an irrepressible urge to preheat your oven, stir some batter, and celebrate a cakeworthy occasion.

3. BOTTLE ROCKET

If you don't know a Cabernet from a Chevrolet, Bottle Rocket is your wine store. Bottle Rocket is designed for people who don't know a lot about wine but won't drink plonk. Every wine is labeled and described, so this is a great place to learn about vintages or to remain happily clueless and still get a wonderful bottle. Unlike any other wine store, Bottle Rocket organizes your choices by food groups. Look for the oversized icons: If you're making a prime porterhouse, head for the red meats. Even take-out meals can be elevated with the right wine; look for the enormous white Chinese food carton. Bottle Rocket has the mood of a toy store—there's even a big chicken in the window. Bring your kids; in the rear of the store is a play area, right next to the extensive wine and cooking library.

4. LE PAIN QUOTIDIEN

The wonder of these bakeries, an international chain, is that they never feel like franchises. While all of them display the signature "look"—lightly waxed pine communal tables—and excellent baked goods, each café also carries its own distinct European charm. At the ABC Carpet branch this includes an outdoor café. Bread and pastries for Le Pain Quotidien are baked on the premises. At the ABC shop you'll see the bakers through a windowed wall. The well-made, crisp-crusted breads include whole wheat, sourdough, walnut boule, five-grain, raisin loaf, and hand-shaped baguettes. Try Le Pain Quotidien's packaged goods—the superb Belgian chocolate-and-hazelnut spread (better than the leading brand), black olives, black olive spreads, and wild mountain capers.

5. LITTLE PIE COMPANY

Arnold Wilkerson and Michael Delaney were obsessed with the traditional American pie: not the kind you sing about, the kind you eat. They traveled cross-country, interviewing grandmothers from Minnesota to California and stopping at county fairs and church socials to sample pies and trade recipes. The culmination of their mutual obsession was opening the Little Pie Company in 1985. Wilkerson and Delaney bake every pie. Our favorites were Personal Peach, Strawberry Rhubarb, Lemon Meringue, Pumpkin, and Sour Cream Apple and Walnut Pie.

6. KITCHEN MARKET

This is the spiciest store on Eighth Avenue. In one part of the store you can buy fantastic burritos; on the other side, you can find all the incendiary ingredients. Kitchen Market carries more than one hundred varieties of chiles, including jalapeños, poblanos, and serranos, all fresh and ranging from lightly spicy to deadly. Some peppers are so hot that special gloves are needed to handle them. Kitchen Market also sells hot sauces. Our choice is Melinda's from Costa Rica; we spread it on broiled fish, toss a few drops into salad dressing, or offer a small dish of it as a dip for bread. We also like the wide selection of freshly made tortillas—spinach, red, white, and whole wheat. Donna Abramson, the proprietor of this charming and well-stocked store, gave us a chile pepper tip: If you ever chomp down on a too-hot pepper, quickly chug a glass of cold milk to cool things down.

7. LA BERGAMOTE

We discovered Bergamote several years ago, when Ninth Avenue and Twenty-first Street was uncharted territory. This corner café, just across the street from the Episcopal Seminary of New York, is a wonderfully peaceful place to stop in the morning for croissants, coffee, and the *New York Times*. The unpretentious exterior of this tiny bakery belies the brilliance inside. Stephan Willemine, the pastry chef, holds a Cap de Patisserie, given only to the most promising pastry chefs. His French pastries are among the best we've found anywhere, France included. The madeleines and financiers are superb, as are the babas au rhum, croissants aux amandes, and tartes aux fruits à l'ancienne.

8. BALDUCCI'S

For many years, Balducci's on Sixth Avenue was a Greenwich Village landmark and reigned as New York City's most famous gourmet food market. In 2003 the family closed the store on Sixth Avenue and turned the lease over to Citarella, a relative newcomer to the city's collection of gourmet emporia. Then, in 2005, Balducci's made a spectacular comeback, opening in a grand old bank building on the corner of West Fourteenth Street. Balducci's was always known for its splendid selection of meat, fish, and Italian foods. The new store certainly picks up where the old one left off. Imagine a food store in a Florentine cathedral and you'll have some sense of Balducci's new space. Visit the café; from there you can admire the architecture and enjoy the lively show of the store.

5

La Bergamote
Phone: (212) 627-9010

7

BALDUCCI'S

FOOD
LOVER'S
MARKET

11 12 1
10 2
9 3
8 4
7 6 5

8

UNION SQUARE GREENMARKET

The Union Square Greenmarket is the centerpiece of New York City's long-term effort to support local agriculture and bring farm-fresh food to city residents. Smaller "greenmarkets" operate in neighborhoods throughout the boroughs, but Union Square is the largest. Mondays, Wednesdays, Fridays, and Saturdays—year-round in every kind of weather—farmers and food artisans from New Jersey, New York, Connecticut, Pennsylvania, and Vermont leave home before dawn and set up their stands on the asphalt walks surrounding the park. Vendors can sell only products they have farmed, produced, caught, or raised themselves, which means you won't find peaches in December, pumpkins in July, or "flash-frozen" Chilean sea bass at any time. This tent city of farm stands sits side by side with the breakdancers, skateboarders, buskers, panhandlers, students, and assorted street characters that congregate in Union Square. The shopping crowd always seems joyful, ranging from preschoolers ogling sunflowers to senior citizens negotiating the price of apples. On weekends, the market feels like a purposeful carnival, sellers hawking their wares, customers squeezing tomato after tomato until someone on line shouts, "Hey, it's a tomato not a car." Union Square is surrounded by a bevy of fine restaurants. Chances are that the hefty fellow next to you rummaging through the garlic ramps is indeed the same cook you've seen on television. Master chefs, accompanied by their assistants, depend on the Greenmarket for local vegetables, fruits, cheeses, poultry, meats—and inspiration. Chef Marco Moreira of Tocqueville, just off the square on Fifteenth Street, arrives first thing in the morning and then again during the day, depending on the menu. Often Marco lets the market decide his specials. At the Greenmarket, you go "ad lib"; leave your shopping list at home. It's all about discovery. Here are a few of our favorite stands, but you'll also find your own and, in so doing, echo the words of Ry Cooder: "If you only look and see / I know you will agree / That the farmer is the man who feeds us all."

BERKSHIRE BERRIES

David Graves and his wife put up their delightful preserves on their Massachusetts farm. They offer standard flavors like raspberry, strawberry, and rhubarb, but if you're feeling adventurous try their garlic, horseradish, or green pepper preserves. The Graveses also sell excellent honey, straight from the beehives they keep on the rooftop of their New York City apartment building. If you want to set up your own hive, David will give you all the details.

BERRIED TREASURE

Franca Tantillo drives her freshly picked blueberries, strawberries, and fraises de bois to New York City from upstate Cook's Falls. When berries are out of season, she brings fingerling and russet potatoes, chives, leeks, and pumpkins.

BLUE MOON FISH

Most commercial fish is taken from the fishing boat to a truck, driven to a central market, and then delivered to your local fish store. Blue Moon's catch comes straight off the boat. Alex and Stephaine Villani fish the waters off eastern Long Island in their steel-hulled trawler Blue Moon and bring the catch right to the Greenmarket. The offerings are seasonal, but you'll find fluke, sea bass, and skate almost all year-round. You won't find fresher fish unless you catch it yourself.

DEEP MOUNTAIN VERMONT MAPLE SYRUP

The owners of Deep Mountain drive 350 miles to bring you their authentic, home-tapped maple syrup and candies.

MARTIN'S PRETZEL

These guys never miss a market. Ten below or 110 degrees in the shade—the Martin's people sell their crisp, salty, home-baked pretzels. Good thing—there are more and more New Yorkers who cannot get through the day without their Martin's Pretzels; we've seen lines form during a blizzard.

$3.00 pound
the french fingerling varie
Buttery flavor some - wax

TARTE TATIN

Autumn is one of the best seasons at the market, especially for apples. In September, October, and into November you'll find just about every variety of apple, crisp and juicy and just off the tree. This version of tarte tatin calls for Jonagolds, but don't limit yourself: Use a different variety every time you make a tart.

6 large Jonagold apples, peeled

6 tablespoons salted butter, at room temperature

½ cup sugar

1 (14-ounce) package classic frozen puff pastry from Dufour, page 54

Crème fraîche (optional)

1   Preheat the oven to 375 degrees.

2   Halve each apple from top to bottom. With a paring knife, cut out the core with all seeds.

3   Put a 9-inch tarte tatin (ovenproof) pan over medium heat and add half of the butter and all of the sugar. Stir with a wooden spoon until the mixture is melted. Place the apples in the pan, alternating cut side up and cut side down.

4   Put little pieces of the remaining butter on top of each apple half. Lower the heat and cook for 15 minutes.

5   Unfold the puff pastry dough, then remove the tarte tatin pan from the heat.

6   Lay the dough on top of the pan, leaving 1 inch of excess dough laying over the outside of the rim, and then crimp with your fingers to form a seal.

7   Bake for 35 to 45 minutes, until the crust is brown on top. Remove from the oven.

8   Take a plate larger than the pan, place it on top of the pan, and invert the tart onto the plate. Wait 5 to 10 minutes before removing the pan. Serve the tart warm with crème fraîche.

CHELSEA MARKET

From the early 1900s to the 1930s, the factories of the National Biscuit Company—inventors of Oreos, Mallomars, Nilla Wafers, and Fig Newtons—dominated two full blocks between Fifteenth and Sixteenth Streets, from Ninth to Eleventh Avenues. Later, as industrial ovens evolved from vertical to horizontal, Nabisco abandoned their huge city facilities and moved to the suburbs. Land was cheap, and one-story buildings were more practical for the new ovens. When Chelsea later became fashionable, a developer bought the old Nabisco buildings, renting the upper lofts to artists, photographers, and media companies. (The Food Network now occupies one block-sized floor.) The ground floor was transformed into Chelsea Market, a corridor with high ceilings, exposed piping, and displays of factory relics. Food stores, restaurants, a flower shop, and a wine store now populate the place where cookies once reigned. Following are some of our frequent stops at Chelsea Market.

Plum Cherry
Sarabeth's
"Spread the Word"
Legendary Spreadable Fruit
Pear Pineapple
Sarabeth's
Legendary Spreadable Fruit
Mixed Berry
Sarabeth's
Chunky Apple
Sarabeth's
Legendary Spreadable Fruit
Plum Cherry
Sarabeth's
Legendary Spreadable Fruit
Pear Pineapple
Sarabeth's
Legendary Spreadable Fruit
Cranberry Relish
Sarabeth's
Legendary Spreadable Fruit
Orange Apricot
Sarabeth's
Legendary Spreadable Fruit
PREMIUM QUALITY

BUON ITALIA

Buon Italia looks like a food warehouse, its wire racks piled high with boxes and cans. This is one of New York's best sources for imported Italian foods. You'll find all the standards—imported pasta, San Marzano tomatoes, wheels of Parmesan. You'll also find exotic delicacies like bottarga, the compressed tuna caviar that we like to shave over simple pastas. Buon Italia carries white truffles in season at very reasonable prices, and, at Christmas, a dozen varieties of panettone, all imported from Italy.

ELENI'S COOKIES

For Eleni, who paints all her cookies by hand, icing is an artist's medium. You can choose from her original designs or bring special requests. She can also print photographs on cookies!

RONNYBROOK FARM DAIRY

Ronnybrook Farm Dairy was founded in 1941 as a conventional dairy. More recently, its mission is to convert city dwellers to real, farm-fresh milk, no relation to the tasteless, overprocessed product sold in supermarkets. Ronnybrook milk—which comes in old-fashioned glass bottles—is pasteurized but not homogenized, so the cream floats to the top. The chocolate milk is terrific, as is the yogurt. Ronnybrook sells almost everything made from milk: ice cream, butter, liquid yogurt, eggnog, cheese yogurt, fromage blanc, and a superb crème fraîche.

LOBSTER PLACE

Founded by Rod and Joan MacGregor in 1974, this shop sells more than a million pounds annually of live lobster, fish, shrimp, shellfish, and squid to restaurants and hotels in the New York area. Here, in the company's retail store, you'll find an alphabet's worth of fresh seafood: Arctic char, bluefish, brook trout, Chilean sea bass, crab cakes, dorade, flounder, gray sole, halibut, lemon sole, mahimahi, mako, marlin, pompano, porgy, red snapper, salmon, shrimp, skate, soft-shell crabs, tilapia, and tuna. The daily selection of oysters offers bivalves from Pebble Beach, Fanny Bay, Wellfleet, Blue Point, and Diamond Point, among others. The Lobster Place will also put together traditional clambakes for your next party—lobster, clams, corn on the cob, and potatoes.

SARABETH'S

Sarabeth and Bill Levine opened their Chelsea Market store to sell the products they've developed at their eponymous New York City restaurants. In the 1980s Sarabeth started making preserves from her grandmother's recipe. Made in small batches without pectin, these preserves are prized for their hand-cut fruit and distinctive bursts of flavor. Among our favorites are blood orange, apricot, pineapple, mixed berry, chunky apple, orange apricot marmalade, and peach apricot. Sarabeth's preserves sometimes upstage her superb baked goods. The glass cabinets of the Chelsea Market store display rugelach, palmiers, and Sarabeth's heart-shaped, chocolate-dipped cookies. Try especially her delicious pumpkin muffins. For holiday dinners, pick up Sarabeth's Budapest Bundt Cake, which weighs in at three and a half pounds and serves twelve people.

10

UPPER EAST SIDE

Generalizations generally don't work when applied to the neighborhoods of New York City, and the Upper East Side is one more proof. While it's often characterized (especially by downtowners) as a bland upscale bedroom community, a sort of Greenwich, Connecticut, South, the Upper East Side definitely has more to offer than its sleepy neighbor to the north. True, the East Side is home to the city's most prestigious apartment buildings, townhouses, mansions, private schools, and private clubs, but it's also home to some of the city's great museums—the Metropolitan, the Guggenheim, the Frick, the Whitney, Neue Galerie—and to some of its best food stores.

While more diverse than some might think, the demographics of the Upper East Side are definitely not downscale: The majority here are well educated and upper middle class.

Editors, writers, media people, bankers, lawyers, doctors, businesspeople, and three quarters of the social register—a sophisticated and demanding group for all things, including food. Which explains why the array of food stores on the Upper East Side is so dazzling. It is remarkable to find so many best-in-class food shops in such a concentrated area. The food stores here have honed their skills and their offerings to accommodate their demanding and affluent customers. But don't be intimidated by all the hype; the store owners here are as friendly and helpful as any we've met.

1. DEBAUVE & GALLAIS

Debauve & Gallais is the oldest and best of the French chocolatiers. Their New York store is a slightly oversized but elegant jewel box. The gold fleur de lys monogram on the window reads: "Fournisseurs des anciens rois de France" (official suppliers to the French royal family). Louis XVI and Marie Antoinette loved the pistoles, wafer-thin gold-embossed chocolate coins. They're still available (the pistoles anyway), and they're amazing with coffee. The tasting room, which looks like a cross between a courtesan's salon and an artist's atelier, is where you'll find the chocolates, shipped daily from France. The chocolate at Debauve & Gallais is high in pure cacao, 60 to 90 percent, with very little sugar or butter, and the result is full flavored and natural. The flavors are original and delightful: Piedmont hazelnut, Perigord nut, Turkish grape, Spanish almond, Bourbon island vanilla, Turin chestnut, and West Indies rum. Open a blue-and-gold box of Debauve & Gallais, inhale the heady smell of pure chocolate, and then savor the texture and the almost overpowering taste. And while the chocolates here may cost an arm and a leg, it's a small sacrifice for one of Marie Antoinette's favorites.

2. ORWASHER'S BAKERY

The Orwasher family have been baking bread at this location since 1916, and after ninety years of practice perfection is an everyday event. The Orwashers were making artisanal bread before artisanal was a word. This is simply one of New York's best bread bakeries. The original brick ovens work night and day, but the store is so quiet and unobtrusive that many people in the neighborhood don't even know it's there. The handmade breads are crusty and delicious. Black bread, challah, cinnamon raisin, corn rye, Irish soda bread, marble, pumpernickel with and without raisins, Russian rye, semolina—and that's only half the list.

3. ITO EN

Ito En, across from Loro Piano, Calypso, and Prada, is a quiet Zen retreat in the midst of the flash of upper Madison Avenue. The tea shop is a long, narrow space of dark polished wood and cool shadows. Ito En is the largest producer of green tea in the world, but everything here is so understated you'll think you're in a provincial Japanese tea shop. Every order unfolds with all the formal grace of a tea ceremony. You choose your tea from a long list of blends and varieties stored along one wall in elegant glass jars. The woman behind the counter takes the time to describe each blend in great detail. She then carefully measures your order onto a scale, and from there into an elegant sack. The tea is handled with great respect, and there is something hypnotic about the care and measured pace of the process. There's also a tea bar where you can sample a wide selection of Ito En's sublime teas. We tried seven varieties of green tea, each one subtly different from the next. You'll find several different oolong and Assam blends, white tea, black tea, and delicious herbal teas blended exclusively by Ito En in Japan. The chocolate-covered almonds sprinkled in green tea powder are a wonderful way to get your chocolate and your antioxidants at the same time. So tear yourself away from Prada, turn off your cell phone, let your credit card cool down, and savor the karma of this serene teahouse.

4. AGATA & VALENTINA

Agata & Valentina is not the title of a Bellini work; it's the name of an Upper East Side market that celebrates food with operatic flair. Everyone here loves what they're doing, and the attitude is contagious. You'd be only half surprised if the workers here started singing in unison. Louis Balducci, one of the partners here, told us that this positive, joyful attitude is no accident, as they hire people they feel will relate well to their customers, then teach them the food business. The sushi chef is from Tibet, the pizza maker from Haiti, and the pasta man is from the Philippines—and they all find a way to communicate their love of food. And the food here is as good as the service. They make the mozzarella by hand, and if you arrive early enough you can watch it happen. The burrata arrives weekly from Corato, Balducci's hometown in Italy. The rest of the cheese collection is extensive, and quite good. Agata & Valentina makes great fresh pasta, which hangs in uncut sheets on wooden racks. The seafood is excellent, bought fresh every day at the new Hunts Point fish market. We saw the fish man trimming a ten-pound sushi-grade tuna with lightning speed. The pizza ovens work all day, turning out thin, crisp-crusted pizza covered with rich San Marzano tomato sauce, buffalo mozzarella, and whatever toppings you might choose. The meat department features prime beef, and on the rotisserie there's excellent roasted chicken; they sell more than two hundred a day. You'll also find some delightful desserts in the bakery; we recommend the banana mousse and the panna cotta. This is a family store, and Balducci and his partner Joe Musco make sure it runs that way. Musco's wife, the real Agata, makes announcements over the PA in a soft Italian accent, and Papa Balducci brings the arugula fresh from his garden.

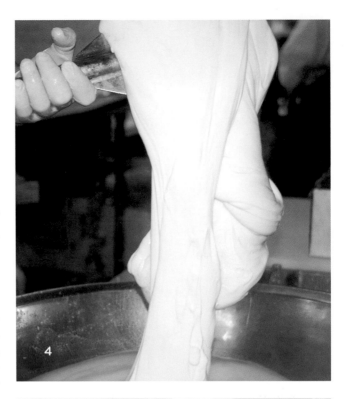

SEAFOOD RISOTTO PRIMAVERA

AGATA & VALENTINA / SERVES 4 TO 6

Here is a very easy risotto recipe, from Agata & Valentina, elegant enough for weekend dining but also casual enough for a quick weeknight supper, and as the name implies it's a perfect introduction to spring.

½ **cup extra-virgin olive oil**

1 **large sweet onion, chopped**

1 **bunch scallions, thinly sliced**

1 **bag cherry tomatoes on the vine, cut in half and seeded**

1 **cup arborio rice**

1 **cup dry white wine**

4 to 6 **cups fish or lobster stock, simmering**

1 **pound rock shrimp, cleaned**

1 **cup shelled or frozen parboiled peas**

2 **tablespoons unsalted butter**

2 **tablespoons chopped fresh flat-leaf parsley**

10 **fresh chives, cut on the bias into thirds**

1   Heat the oil in a large sauté pan over medium-high heat and add the onion, scallions, and tomatoes.

2   Cook, stirring, until the vegetables are softened, about 5 minutes.

3   Add the rice and stir to coat with the oil for about 1 minute.

4   Add the wine and raise the heat slightly; cook, stirring constantly, until the alcohol has evaporated.

5   Turn the heat back down to medium and add the simmering stock, one ladleful at a time, stirring gently but continuously. When the bottom of the pan gets a little dry, add another ladleful of stock and stir until all the liquid is absorbed.

6   After 15 minutes, add the shrimp and peas and continue pouring in stock and stirring until the shrimp just turns opaque and the stock is absorbed.

7   Fold in the butter, stirring gently until it just melts. Sprinkle with parsley and chives and serve immediately.

4

5. LEONARDI'S

Some stores are good at fish, others are good at meat; Leonardi's is very good at both. This family business started life as a fish store in 1910. Later the family bought out a German butcher shop and merged it with the fish store. The result is the best fish store–butcher shop in New York. On one side of the store are the fish, buried in pristine ice, bright-eyed and fresh. The poached shrimp and crab cakes are excellent. The butcher shop at the back of the store sells only prime beef and veal, dry aged in their specially built meat locker. What makes this store special is the execution. They do everything with remarkable precision and care.

ROASTED SALMON

LEONARDI'S / SERVES 6

Even if you've never cooked before you can't go wrong with this recipe. It's incredibly easy, and incredibly good. Not a lot of work for a great weeknight dinner. The secret ingredient here is Jane's Crazy Mixed-up Salt, a delicious and secret combination that adds a special zip to fish. If you can't find Jane's salt at your grocer, order it online.

Olive oil

2 pounds salmon fillet, with skin

2 lemons

½ cup soy sauce

½ cup rice-wine vinegar

2 tablespoons Jane's Crazy Mixed-up Salt

6 scallions, finely chopped

1 Preheat the oven to 350 degrees.

2 Line a baking dish with aluminum foil and spray it with oil.

3 Place the salmon, skin side down, in the baking pan. Squeeze 1 of the lemons over the salmon.

4 In a small bowl, whisk together the soy sauce and vinegar and pour it over the fish.

5 Sprinkle with Jane's Crazy Mixed-up Salt and the scallions.

6 Close the foil around the salmon by crimping the edges together.

7 Bake for 30 minutes, opening the foil for the last 10 to 15 minutes of baking, until the salmon flakes easily when prodded with a fork. Serve on a platter with slices of the remaining lemon.

6. LADY M

Take twenty crêpes, a bowl of chantilly and vanilla custard, and try to make a perfectly round cake only three inches thick. Or go to Lady M and buy one of their signature Mille Crêpes; it is light, airy, and delicious. This very simple East Side bakery makes some of the most beautiful cakes we've seen anywhere. They are all made by hand, and every one is a remarkable combination of baker's craft and chef's sensibility. We tried several of the cakes and especially liked the Montague de Fraise, a meringue-topped strawberry tart; the gâteau aux marrons, with chestnut puree and whipped cream; and potiron mousse, a froth of pumpkin and cream. The gâteau New Yorkais is like no other cheesecake you've tried.

GÂTEAU DE CRÊPES

LADY M / SERVES 10

This is your chance to try to match the skill of Lady M's master bakers. We'll warn you now: This is not easy. The toughest part here is the dexterity required to stack one layer evenly on top of the next. Use a form and don't be afraid to use a sharp knife to trim the edges.

FOR THE BATTER

6 tablespoons unsalted butter

3 cups milk

6 large eggs

1½ cups all-purpose flour

7 tablespoons sugar

Pinch of salt

FOR THE PASTRY CREAM

2 cups milk

1 vanilla bean, halved and scraped

6 large egg yolks

½ cup sugar

⅓ cup cornstarch, sifted

3½ tablespoons unsalted butter

FOR ASSEMBLING THE CAKE

Corn oil

2 cups heavy cream

1 tablespoon granulated sugar, or more if necessary

3 tablespoons kirsch

Confectioners' sugar

The day before you plan to serve the crêpes, make the batter and the pastry cream.

MAKE THE BATTER

1   In a small saucepan, cook the butter until brown like hazelnuts. Set aside.

2   In another small pan, heat the milk until steaming; remove from the heat and let cool for 10 minutes.

3   With a mixer on medium-low speed, beat together the eggs, flour, sugar, and salt.

4   Slowly add the hot milk and browned butter.

5   Pour into a container with a spout, cover, and refrigerate overnight.

MAKE THE PASTRY CREAM

1   Bring the milk with the vanilla bean and its seeds to a boil, then remove from the heat and set aside for 10 minutes; remove the vanilla bean.

2   Fill a large bowl with ice and set aside a small bowl that can hold the finished pastry cream and be placed in this ice bath.

3   In a medium-size heavy-bottomed pan, whisk together the egg yolks, sugar, and cornstarch. Gradually whisk in the hot milk, then place the pan over high heat and bring to a boil, whisking vigorously for 1 to 2 minutes.

4   Press the pastry cream through a fine-mesh sieve into the small bowl. Set the bowl in the ice bath and stir until the temperature of the pastry cream reaches 140 degrees on an instant-read thermometer.

5   Stir in the butter. When completely cool, cover and refrigerate overnight.

ASSEMBLE THE CAKE

1   Bring the batter to room temperature. Place a nonstick or seasoned 9-inch crêpe pan over medium heat. Swab the surface with oil, then add about 3 tablespoons of the batter and swirl to cover the surface.

2   Cook until the bottom just begins to brown, about 1 minute, then carefully lift an edge and flip the crêpe with your fingers.

3   Cook on the other side for no longer than 5 seconds. Flip the crêpe onto a baking sheet lined with parchment. Repeat until you have 20 perfect crêpes.

4   Pass the pastry cream through a sieve once more.

5   Whip the heavy cream together with the granulated sugar and the kirsch until thick; it won't hold peaks.

6   Fold the whipped cream into the pastry cream.

7   Lay 1 crêpe on a cake plate. Using an icing spatula, completely cover with a thin layer of pastry cream (about ¼ cup). Cover with a second crêpe and repeat to make a stack of 20, with the best-looking crêpe on top.

8   Chill for at least 2 hours.

9   Let the cake sit at room temperature for 30 minutes before serving. If you have a blowtorch, sprinkle the top crêpe with 2 tablespoons sugar and caramelize with the torch; otherwise, dust with confectioners' sugar. Slice like a cake and serve.

7. DYLAN'S CANDY BAR

What her father did for the tweed suit, Dylan Lauren is doing for the candy store. She's combined a strong sense of design and the ability to create an alternate reality around everyday products. This is not candyland, it's candy universe. The store is enormous, and every cubic centimeter is devoted to, well, candy, much of it over-scale. The ground floor is dominated by giant lollipops, ornate candy topiary, and the colors, garish anywhere else, here make delightful eye candy. On display is every color of M&M, gumdrop, and jelly bean. Giant milk and white chocolate bunnies hop through candy foliage. One whole wall is devoted to chocolate-covered things: raisins, peanuts, cherries, malted milk balls. You'll find cotton candy, Sugar Daddies, Pez, gum balls, licorice, Necco Wafers; candies that look like rings, whistles, bracelets, necklaces; candy canes, gummy bears, gummy worms, gumdrops, and an ice-cream counter and a cupcake display. The stairs to the lower floor are clear plastic filled with gummy bears, and down those stairs is the Candy Hall of Fame, featuring candy choices of the rich and celebrated. And if your kids aren't spoiled enough by the visit you can rent the place out for a birthday party. The decor changes to match the holidays, and it's worth a visit just to see the seasonal changes. This place is pure sugar and pure fun.

8. SABLE'S SMOKED FISH

Kenny Sze perfected his smoked fish skills as the head of Zabar's fish department before he set off on his own and opened Sable's. The result is excellent smoked salmon, sable, and sturgeon, perfectly cut and trimmed. It's obvious that Kenny didn't waste time or money on interior design or graphics; the spartan store borrows its decorative motif from a monastery, and all the signs are handwritten on the same paper that wraps the fish. The focus here is on the fish, just the fish. This single-mindedness shows in the quality of the food. Sable's offers excellent lobster salad, smoked lake sturgeon, eastern Gaspé salmon, gravlax salmon with dill, whitefish, smoked mackerel fillets, smoked tuna, smoked Scottish kippers, poached salmon, and more.

9. SHERRY-LEHMANN

Sherry-Lehmann, a cross between a wine shop and an investment bank, is one of New York's oldest and best wine shops. Back when businessmen were wading through three-martini lunches, Sherry-Lehmann was one of the first stores to take wine seriously, and the foresight has paid off. A bottle of 1945 Mouton Rothschild, worth less than five dollars back then, now fetches twelve thousand dollars, and there's a good chance Sherry-Lehmann still has a few cases in its remarkable cellar. The selection here is vast and well chosen; the Bordeaux and Burgundy sections are encyclopedic. A big business here is wine futures, the buying and selling of vintages on speculation before they come out, in the hopes that once on the market values will increase. Here's a shopping tip next time your significant other gets impatient as you riffle the racks at Barney's: Send him across the street to Sherry-Lehmann, where there's a good chance he'll spend more than you.

10

10

11

EAT
(Is Owned By The Zabar Inc.)

11

10. PAYARD PATISSERIE

François Payard was born into the pastry business. His parents founded Au Nid des Friandises, in Nice, a classic French pastry store. After stints at Lucas Carton, Le Bernardin, and Daniel, Payard opened his own patisserie and restaurant on the Upper East Side. Payard is a café/patisserie after the European model; patrons are welcome to sit for as long as they like, chatting, reading a book, or just staring off into space. The café is at the front of the store, the restaurant in back. There's a chocolate bar, a coffee bar, a pastry counter, and a small selection of sandwiches, including an excellent croque monsieur. The tarts are word-of-mouth popular among New York's French community, and the croissants and coffee are excellent. One other favorite here is the galette des rois. It's a special almond cake made for the Feast of the Assumption. A small charm, usually the figure of a king, is baked inside the cake. The cake is sliced, and the youngest member of the family goes under the table and decides who in the family gets which slice. Everyone bites into his or her slice, carefully, hoping to find the embedded king. The one who gets the slice with the charm is named king or queen for the evening, complete with cardboard crown, and gets to pick a co-monarch. Other great pastries here are the Mont Blanc, the éclair, the Paris Brest, and the banana and lemon tart. The breakfast pastries are also very good; we liked the kugelhopf and the cannele de Bordeaux.

11. E.A.T.

While we're not sure whether the Eli Zabar saga would be better as a book or a made-for-TV movie, we do have a title: *East of Fifth*. That's where this son of the West Side's most esteemed food family created a culinary empire of his own, which includes E.A.T., Eli's Vinegar Factory, Eli's, and Eli's Bread, all on the Upper East Side. Zabar's first store was E.A.T., a small bakery and café offering homemade salads and sandwiches in the Rhinelander Mansion on Madison and Seventy-second. The business thrived, and Zabar never stopped expanding his business. He eventually left Seventy-second to move to a much larger restaurant café. The place is always packed. At the counter you'll see East Side matrons, moms, nannies, a smattering of tourists, and, in summer, a few East Side bankers left to fend for themselves, looking lost. The breads here are all baked by Zabar and excellent. The salads are superb. The chicken salad is the best we've tried anywhere, and the new potato and whitefish salads are delicious. The precooked roast chicken served with long strips of carrot and potato makes a great quick winter dinner. We can also recommend the pot roast, which comes with a red gravy and roasted potatoes. This is comfort food done to perfection. The baked goods here, the cakes, the pies, the tarts, the cookies, are all excellent, though some people may find spending twelve dollars for a bag of six cookies a bit excessive.

10

12

12

12

12. ELI'S VINEGAR FACTORY

Zabar's next move was up to Ninety-first Street, where he opened Eli's Vinegar Factory. A precursor to Whole Foods and Gourmet Garage, Vinegar Factory was the first gourmet mega-supermarket. New York always had gourmet markets, places like Balducci's and Zabar's, but nothing on the scale of the Vinegar Factory, which occupies the ninety-thousand-square-foot factory building at 431 East Ninety-first Street. Everything at the Vinegar Factory is first quality: dairy/cheese, bread, pastry, meat, fish, produce, appetizing/smoked fish, and coffee. There's a rooftop greenhouse where the store grows its own tomatoes, lettuce, and herbs. There's a prepared foods section that offers many of the same things as E.A.T. plus a lot more; the green beans are always perfect, as are the egg salad and the Tuscan bread soup. People don't come to the Vinegar Factory to buy a quart of milk. This is an all-day, all-in-one food shopping experience. Eli's Manhattan on Third Avenue and Eightieth Street is a smaller clone of the Vinegar Factory. In the building next door to the Vinegar Factory is Eli's bakery, which turns out all the baked goods sold in all of Eli's stores, and under the Eli's label all over the country. Eli's bread has become a contender for best in New York. The voting is not in yet, but we can tell you it's up there with the very best. Our favorites are the raisin pecan loaf and the country loaf, and the rugelach and biscotti are also top notch. The heat from the bakery ovens warms the rooftop greenhouse. Eli's is a bakery on the verge of becoming an ecosystem. In one of the Ninety-first Street buildings they make dough for the croissants that is folded on a special machine and then carried next door to be baked. Don't miss the cookie section, with excellent palmiers and shortbread, and if you feel like cooking buy some of the ready-made dough—chocolate shortbread, sweet pastry dough, or puff pastry dough. Zabar has led a one-man food crusade on the Upper East Side, and the results have been outstanding.

12

MUSHROOM BARLEY SOUP

ELI'S VINEGAR FACTORY / SERVES 6 TO 8

Mushroom barley soup is one of those foods that epitomizes the word "comfort." In New York, it's also synonymous with Eli Zabar's E.A.T. and The Vinegar Factory. Once you've had their version you will be compelled to return time and time again. It's quite simply the best in town and has become a special wintertime favorite. Their recipe also happens to be very simple to make at home. The veal stock is the only tricky part, but it's the key to this soup's special savor. If you'd rather not make stock from scratch, you can pick up some of The Vinegar Factory's house-made varieties.

Salt and freshly ground black peper to taste

2 cups raw barley

4 tablespoons unsalted butter

2 cups diced yellow onion

2 cups finely chopped leeks (white part only)

1 cup sliced white mushrooms

1 tablespoon chopped fresh thyme leaves

1½ quarts chicken stock

2 cups light veal stock

1 tablespoon chopped fresh dill (optional)

1   Bring a large pot of salted water to a boil. Add barley and cook until soft, about 10 minutes. Drain and set aside.

2   Melt the butter in a deep, heavy-bottomed pot over low heat. Add the onions and leeks. Sauté until they are very soft, stirring occasionally, about 15 minutes. Do not allow them to brown.

3   Add the mushrooms and thyme, increase the heat to medium, and cook just until the mushrooms begin to soften and release their liquid.

4   Add both stocks and the drained barley to the pot. Bring to a simmer and cook uncovered for about 20 minutes, to marry the flavors.

5   Taste the soup and season with salt and pepper as needed. Serve in warmed bowls, topping each with a sprinkling of dill, if desired.

13. LOBEL'S MEATS

Lobel's is the Fabergé of meat. The best, the biggest, and the most expensive, and they make no bones about it. They've been at the same location since 1930, and five generations have carried the business forward. These butchers really know meat. Walk into the store and you'll marvel at how they've managed to squeeze so many cleavers, knives, chopping blocks, sharpening steels, meat grinders, bone saws, and beefy butchers into one tiny space. But the real marvel here is the meat. First Lobel's selects all their cuts from prime, the highest grade. One of the butchers explained that prime beef has a soft reddish bone and a thin web of fat running through it, the marbling. The butcher at Lobel's buys only the top of the prime, which is scarce and difficult to identify. They dry age the meat for four to six weeks in a temperature-controlled locker at between thirty-one and thirty-eight degrees. The aging process breaks down the connective tissue, which makes the meat tender, and when the meat loses over 30 percent of its moisture the result is a more concentrated flavor. The costly aging process and the ensuing weight loss explain, at least partially, why Lobel's prices are so high. Lobel's also sells prime veal and lamb, Berkshire pork, and poultry. Cook a cut from Lobel's and you'll realize that what the butchers have been spouting isn't hype. The meat is sensational, tender, and full of flavor, up there with the best we've ever tasted. For a memorable roast the capons are also amazingly flavorful, with a slightly stronger taste than chicken. So hold your breath, ignore the prices, plunk down a chunk of change for a couple of steaks, and for one night turn your kitchen into the best steakhouse in New York. Lobel's Web site is complete and highly informative, and the store will ship just about anywhere.

QUAIL WITH CREAMY HERB SAUCE AND LEMONY COUSCOUS

LOBEL'S MEATS / SERVES 6

If you've never had quail this is the perfect recipe to start with. Quail is a little gamier than chicken or duck, and the seasonings in the recipe bring out the flavor of the bird without emphasizing the stronger taste. This is Lobel's own recipe, from its award-winning cookbook. It is easy to make and quite original, and the result is an outstanding and sophisticated dinner.

FOR THE MARINADE

½ **cup olive oil**

1 clove garlic, crushed

1 tablespoon chopped fresh thyme

1 tablespoon chopped fresh rosemary

1 tablespoon chopped fresh flat-leaf parsley

2 teaspoons sweet Hungarian paprika

Freshly ground black pepper to taste

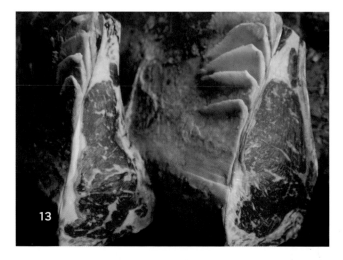

13

FOR THE QUAIL

12 (3- to 4-ounce) partially boned quail

1 cup chicken stock

1 tablespoon sweet Hungarian paprika

¼ cup heavy cream

2 teaspoons unsalted butter

1 teaspoon minced fresh thyme

1 teaspoon minced fresh rosemary

1 teaspoon minced fresh flat-leaf parsley

Salt and freshly ground black pepper to taste

Juice of ½ lemon

FOR THE COUSCOUS

2 cups couscous

¼ cup fresh lemon juice

3 tablespoons unsalted butter

2 tablespoons minced fresh flat-leaf parsley

Salt and freshly ground black pepper to taste

MAKE THE MARINADE

1 In a small bowl, combine all the ingredients and whisk to blend.

MAKE THE QUAIL

1 Lay the quail in a baking dish and pour the marinade over them. Turn the quail and gently rub the mixture into the meat.

2 Cover and refrigerate for at least 6 hours and up to 24 hours.

3 Preheat the broiler.

4 In a small saucepan, combine the stock and paprika and bring to a boil over high heat. Reduce the heat to medium and simmer rapidly for 15 to 20 minutes, or until reduced by half.

5 Add the cream and bring to a boil. Reduce the heat and simmer until slightly thickened. Stir in the butter and herbs until the butter melts. Season to taste with salt and pepper.

6 Meanwhile, lift the quail from the marinade and pat dry with paper towels. Lay the quail, breast side up, on a rack set on a broiler pan.

7 Broil for 5 to 6 minutes on each side, or until the quail is golden brown on the outside and opaque throughout.

MAKE THE COUSCOUS

1 In a small saucepan, bring 2 cups water to a boil.

2 Put the couscous, lemon juice, and butter in a medium bowl and pour the boiling water over it. Stir, cover, and let stand for 8 to 10 minutes, or until the liquid is absorbed.

3 Fluff the couscous with a fork, stir in the parsley, and season with salt and pepper. Spoon the couscous onto a serving platter and top with the quail. Spoon the sauce over the quail and drizzle with lemon juice.

14. SANT AMBROEUS

Everything in this café/restaurant is so authentically Italian most people who haven't been to Italy think it's French. Sant Ambroeus looks like it was flown in from Milan and reassembled on Madison Avenue, with none of the clichés of Americanized Italian decor. The stand-up front counter is a great place to have a cappuccino and panino. The foam on the cappuccino is perfect every time, and the crowd is eclectic and attractive. You'll see kids from the uptown private schools stopping in after three for gelato, East Side matrons coming in for dinner at six, plus gallery owners, plastic surgeons, museum curators, and couturiers lining the counter at all hours. The cookies and gelatos are made only with fresh seasonal fruit, and Sant Ambroeus's Christmas cake is an event unto itself, wrapped in beautiful reddish pink paper. The tarts are a must, as is the dolce de Verona, made with chocolate sponge cake and raspberry jam. This is Milano on Madison.

15. WILLIAM GREENBERG

The legend is that in 1945 William Greenberg, an army cook, won enough money playing gin rummy with his fellow soldiers to open his bakery. The store has flourished since then and has become an Upper East Side institution. So much so that when Judy Adler bought the business from Greenberg the only thing she changed was the address, moving from Third Avenue to Madison. Everything else stayed the same: the menu, the cooks, the recipes. There are probably only eight or nine people on the whole Upper East Side who have not had a birthday cake made by Greenberg's. The window display hasn't changed either: tin bakery trays on white paper brimming with cookies. Their linzer tortes and black-and-white cookies are world famous. The glaze on the black-and-whites is flawless and delicious. Cookies cover every inch of the small, functional space. The schnecken, made from a sour cream yeast dough rolled up with raisins, pecans, brown sugar, and cinnamon, are unusual and good. William Greenberg's good luck at cards was a windfall to New York's cookie lovers.

14

15

15

15

15

16. SCHALLER & WEBER

Yorkville runs from Eightieth to Ninetieth Streets east of Lexington Avenue. Until a few years ago it was called Germantown, home to the largest German community in the city. German restaurants, beer halls, butchers, and delicatessens lined Eighty-sixth Street from Lexington to the East River. But, slowly, as real estate values increased, first- and second-generation German families were displaced by young professionals, and one by one the German stores have slowly disappeared. Today only a few remain. One of our favorites, Elk Candy, closed while we were putting this book together. Fortunately Schaller & Weber, one of the best sausage makers in the world, has survived and thrived. Germany is supposed to be the sausage capital of the world, but every year Schaller & Weber enters sausage competitions all over Europe and consistently brings back the bacon. This is no surprise; the knockwurst, bratwurst, liverwurst, and cervelet (a German salami) deserve their august reputation. The most popular sausage here is the bockwurst, very mild, and made from veal and pork. Other attractions are the salads, three kinds of potato: German, German with bacon, and American. They're all good, but we especially loved the German potato salad. Their signature salad is the meat salad, made with julienned strips of beef, pork, and veal tossed with pickles, celery, and mayonnaise. This holdover from the old Yorkville has become world famous, and deservedly so.

11

UPPER WEST SIDE

The Upper West Side is easily the greenest neighborhood in New York, bounded on the east by Central Park and the west by the wide swath of Riverside Park and the Hudson River. It's bounded on the south by Fifty-ninth Street and the north by 125th, and encompasses the hilly beauty of Morningside Park.

The apartment buildings along Central Park West and Riverside Drive are superb examples of prewar residential architecture. The side streets are lined with beautifully preserved four- and five-story townhouses, and everywhere you look you'll find great food stores, from the tiniest bodega to sprawling hypermarkets.

Although the Upper West Side shares Central Park with the Upper East Side, that and the weather about cover what the two neighborhoods have in common. Even if some long-term West Siders complain that their neighborhood has become too gentrified, the mix here is still eclectic. The West Side is intellectual and artistic, gritty and colorful, European and Latin, down to earth, in touch with its ethnic roots.

From Columbus Circle to Columbia University, this area is more diverse racially, religiously, and economically than its neighbor on the other side of the park. The food stores reflect this diversity. The Victoria, a Chinese-Cuban restaurant on Broadway, is a fun place to eat and a wonderful metaphor for the entire West Side food scene. On the Upper West Side, hundred-year-old appetizing stores stand comfortably next to trendy new bakeries. Each new generation has left its stamp on the community. The good thing is that while individuals may move on, the food stores they've created still flourish.

1. OPPENHEIMER PRIME MEATS

Robert Pence, who bought this venerable shop from Harry Oppenheimer, is one of New York's most erudite butchers. He studied at the Culinary Institute and later worked under the tutelage of Daniel Boulud and Jean-Georges Vongerichten, two of New York's star chefs. Oppenheimer meats are all prime and aged. In addition, Oppenheimer sells 36,000 chickens, 1,000 Thanksgiving turkeys, and an incalculable number of July Fourth hamburgers.

3

4

4

6

3. MURRAY'S STURGEON

Murray's Sturgeon has been selling smoked salmon, sturgeon, whitefish, chubs, kippered salmon, and a great selection of flavored cream cheeses for more than fifty years. This is a spare, no-nonsense store with efficient, helpful service. It's reassuring to know that, anywhere you go on the Upper West Side, you are within close reach of a quarter pound of smoked salmon.

4. BARNEY GREENGRASS

The Upper West Side absorbed three waves of Jewish immigration: at the turn of the twentieth century, and before and after World War II. One effect of this triple influx is the highest concentration of smoked fish vendors in the world. Though very different in ambience, the two best sources—Barney Greengrass and Murray's Sturgeon—are located within blocks of each other in the West Eighties. Barney Greengrass has been at the same location since 1908; the roster of devoted customers is a Who's Who of New Yorkiana. Barney Greengrass, a.k.a. the Sturgeon King, has been featured in so many travel books that, on any day, you will hear tourists from all over the world mouth his mantra: "Lox 'n' eggs." Gary Greengrass, grandson of the original owner, is just as passionate about the business and the quality of the food. As you enter, the long counter at right is your destination for world-class sturgeon and chopped liver. To your left is the restaurant, furnished with green Formica tables and aluminum chairs that look like they've been lifted from a 1950s sitcom. Aside from the smoked fish and chopped liver, our other favorites are the borscht, great with a spoonful of sour cream, and the kugel— noodle pudding. Anybody who comes to New York should make a pilgrimage to this legendary spot, meet Gary Greengrass, and sit down for a "nice piece of fish."

5. MARGOT PATISSERIE

In its early days, the Ansonia apartment building was a vertical artist's colony that housed singers, painters, musicians, dancers, poets, and Babe Ruth. It featured a rooftop farm complete with cows and goats. Later in its celebrated history, the Ansonia's ornate swimming pool and baths were the site of New York's most celebrated sex clubs, the Continental Baths and Plato's Retreat. Now a pricey condominium, the Ansonia's tenants are more likely to be investment bankers than transvestites or tenors. Architecturally, the Ansonia, with its elaborate, all-white contours and fanciful decorations, is a prime example of what Frank Lloyd Wright once called the "Frenchite Pastry School." The perfect place for a bakery: Margot Patisserie is hidden behind an art nouveau window in the rabbit warren of the Ansonia's ground floor. The ambience is pure Paris, as are the croissants, pains aux chocolat, tarte tatin, apricot tart, and quiche. But the real draw is the clafouti custard. Margot's clafouti is the quintessential version— perfect, light, and packed with whole cherries.

6. ABSOLUTE BAGELS

At a time when any piece of dough with a hole poked through it can be called a bagel, Absolute Bagels makes the authentic item—hand-rolled from high-gluten flour, yeast, and malt, then boiled and baked. The result is perfection. Crunchy outside, chewy inside, with a distinct woody taste. The master behind this Olympian bagel is Sam Thonkrieng, born in Thailand. Sam worked in several bagel bakeries and later bought Absolute from the original owner. He saw the shortcuts that other bagel makers were taking and resolved to do things right. Absolute is the Greenwich clock of bagels, the standard for all other bagels.

Chocolate Chip
Walnut Cookie
$3.50

Dark Chocolate
Peanut Butter Chip
Cookie $3.50

7. LEVAIN BAKERY

Cookie monsters young and old have come to know and love Levain Bakery on the Upper West Side. Levain's "monster" cookies are about an inch thick and weigh in at eight ounces each. These big cookies—dark chocolate, chocolate chip, walnut, oatmeal raisin, and peanut butter chip—look like scones and taste like cake. But if Levain wants to call them cookies, we'll go along. They're delicious.

8. FAIRWAY

Fairway is a megamarket con brio. Each of these vast stores is wired into New York's human energy grid, humming and crackling with activity. The crowds flow in and out, moving continuously from street into store and out again. Shopping at Fairway is a constant town meeting, with complete strangers discussing the quality of the grapefruit or the bargains in the cheese department. The swarms of shoppers circulate around vibrant hills of fruit and vegetables, pyramids of olive oil cans, architectural follies made of chocolate bars. There's always a sense of fun; at the Harlem store, shoppers don store-issued anoraks to enter the meat lockers. Fairway is committed to delivering the highest quality foods at the lowest possible prices. In addition to the fantastic produce, fresh bread, health foods, and vast selection of cheeses, Fairway also sells selected products, like virgin olive oil, under its own label. Fairway's newest location is in a beautiful old Brooklyn warehouse. Take the trip, if only to visit the café, which features a stunning view of lower Manhattan and the Statue of Liberty.

9. CRUMBS BAKE SHOP

Cupcake stores have been popping up in New York City with all the verve of dot-coms in the 1990s. When Mia and Jason Bauer opened Crumbs in 2003, it was the West Side's first cupcake shop, and their delightful confections caught on quickly. Mia and Jason bake more than thirty-six varieties, a total of twelve to fifteen thousand cupcakes weekly. They also produce more than one hundred custom-made cakes. We like the Oreo cupcake—chocolate cake with vanilla buttercream frosting, with crushed Oreos mixed in the frosting and large Oreo chunks sprinkled on top.

9

SIMPLE CUPCAKES

CRUMBS BAKE SHOP /

MAKES 24 LARGE CUPCAKES OR 36 MINIS

Everyone has a favorite cupcake recipe. Everyone thinks theirs is the best. But we'll put this one from Susan's personal cookbook up against all challengers. These cupcakes can be dipped in coconut, chocolate chips, sprinkles, M&M's, peanut butter chips, cookie crumbs, or just about anything else.

2 cups all-purpose flour

¼ teaspoon salt

1 teaspoon baking soda

½ cup (1 stick) plus 1 tablespoon unsalted butter, at room temperature

1½ cups sugar

2 teaspoons vanilla extract

3 large eggs

1 cup whole milk

Basic Buttercream Frosting (recipe follows)

1   Preheat the oven to 350 degrees.

2   Butter two muffin pans or line the cups with paper cupcake liners.

3   Sift together the flour, salt, and baking soda and set aside.

4   With an electric mixer, cream the butter, sugar, and vanilla.

5   Add the eggs one at a time, beating well after each addition.

6   Gradually add the dry ingredients and then the milk. Beat until smooth.

7   Fill the cupcake cups with batter three quarters full.

8   Bake for 30 minutes, or until a toothpick inserted in the center comes out clean. Let cool completely

BASIC BUTTERCREAM FROSTING

2½ cups confectioners' sugar

½ cup (1 stick) salted butter, at room temperature

1½ teaspoons vanilla extract

2 tablespoons milk

1   Combine the confectioners' sugar and butter in the bowl of an electric mixer and beat until fluffy.

2   Add the vanilla and milk and beat again until combined; do not overbeat.

3   Spread on top of the cooled cupcakes.

10. ZABAR'S

Which came first? Zabar's or the Upper West Side? Zabar's opened in 1934, but for many New Yorkers and tourists their first discovery of the special West Side zeitgeist started with a trip to Zabar's. It is more than a store; it's a life experience. The first time you go there you may be overwhelmed by the rush and noise of the crowd and by the overflowing displays. Breathe deeply and center yourself. Soon the wonders of Zabar's will come into focus. First, the smoked fish counter. Take a ticket, and wait for the counterman to call your number. Meanwhile, survey the fish inside the glass case—eastern Nova, western Nova, Scotch salmon, whitefish, chubs, sturgeon, and several types of pickled herring. No matter how many people are waiting, the counterman will give you a couple of tastes. Some countermen will flirt or joke (in English, Yiddish, or Korean); other countermen are silent, their attention on their long, thin knives and the fish fillet before them. Next, follow your nose to the coffee section. Zabar's roasts and grinds its own. You can choose whole beans or have the coffee ground to your specs. The Colombian Supreme, Kenya AA, and the Double Dark Espresso were our favorites. Still on the first floor, head for the ample cheese section, the bakery, the prepared foods counter, and the butcher. If kitchen equipment and housewares are of interest, climb the stairs to the second floor. The selection is awesome. We counted a dozen different espresso machines. Even if your cooking is limited to the microwave, you'll find some enchanting gadget or machine.

CRÈME CAFÉ

ZABAR'S / SERVES 4

This traditional dessert recipe takes full advantage of Zabar's superb house-roasted coffee. Pick your favorite blend and whip up a delicious batch of this rich custard.

2 cups sugar

⅓ cup coffee brewed from Zabar's special blend beans, at room temperature

3 large whole eggs plus 3 large yolks

3 cups whole milk

1   Preheat the oven to 350 degrees.

2   In a saucepan, heat 1 cup of the sugar with 1 tablespoon water and cook until it turns light amber.

3   Pour the syrup into a 10- or 12-inch soufflé mold, and swirl the mold to coat the bottom with the syrup.

4   In a bowl, mix together the remaining sugar, coffee, eggs, and egg yolks.

5   Warm the milk (do not let it boil) and slowly pour over the mixture, mixing constantly with a wooden spoon.

6   Pour the liquid in the soufflé mold.

7   Place the mold in a deep baking dish and fill the dish with hot water so that the water comes halfway up the side of the mold.

8   Bake for 45 minutes to 1 hour, until a knife inserted in the center comes out clean. Let cool completely. Put a plate on the top of the mold and invert to remove the crème café.

CHAPTER 12

BRONX

The area around Arthur Avenue in the Bronx is Little Italy North, and it shares a lot of the same history with its older sibling to the south. Italian immigrants settled in the area in the early twentieth century, creating an enclave of Italian grocers, salumerias, cheese stores, and restaurants, all centered around Our Lady of Mount Carmel Church. Over the years, as the immigrant families became more prosperous and they moved out to greener suburbs, they were replaced by Albanians, Mexicans, and Russians. But while Manhattan's Little Italy is more a memory than a reality, its larger part swallowed up by an ever-expanding Chinatown, the stores of Arthur Avenue remain stalwartly Italian, run by the second and third generations of the families who founded them. Italian families from all over the region come back to Arthur Avenue and their roots—at least for an afternoon of shopping.

It's hard to find really good mesamanich sausage in Darien.

These returnees and the new immigrant communities have kept the stores of Arthur Avenue thriving. More recently they've been discovered by the food cognoscenti, so that on a weekday morning you just might spot a few world-famous chefs poking around the shops of Arthur Avenue searching out the best ingredients for their next brilliant pasta.

Mount Carmel is the best place to start your exploration, and as you wander down Arthur Avenue you will be delighted by the quality of the food and the exuberance of the people.

1. TEITEL BROTHERS

Teitel's is where the gourmet branch of an end-of-the-world cult might come to stock up. Here you can find fifty-gallon tins of extra-virgin cold-pressed Italian olive oil, fifty-pound sacks of flour, and tomato puree by the pound—enough to make pasta for the entire population of Noah's Ark. Teitel's is more of a restaurant supplier, but they are glad to sell to the general public.

2. MADONIA BROTHERS BAKERY

The feature here is great bread, made by hand and baked in the store's own wood-burning ovens. The windows and shelves are filled with freshly baked bread—prosciutto bread, provolone bread, cranberry and walnut bread, pane di casa. In keeping with the changes in the neighborhood, this Italian-owned bakery is staffed by Albanian women in starched white aprons, and the service is excellent. To help you decide which of its great breads you like best, Madonia Brothers leaves out a tray of samples for its customers.

MIKE'S DELI

MIKE'S DELI

3

3. BORGATTI'S RAVIOLI & EGG NOODLES

Down the block from the market, facing the church, is a store with a window full of American flags, a statue of the Virgin Mary, and very little evidence that this is one of the best ravioli stores in New York. Inside, every inch of space is taken up by religious images, family pictures, and drying pasta. Spaghetti hangs from the ceiling. Trays of ravioli are everywhere. Imagine a pasta factory on a small boat. To perform any task, something must be moved. The pasta machines, all vintage models, are stowed in the back of the store and rolled out one at a time for each step of the process. The proprietor, Mario Borgatti, took over his parents' business twenty years ago and never left. All of the staff are long-timers. One of the pasta makers we met has been working in the store for over twenty years. And the experience shows in the quality of the beautifully made pasta and ravioli. The texture is perfect, and the ravioli fillings are amazingly light and flavorful. These hardworking craftsmen turn out a superb product, a must try. Of course they're closed Sundays.

PAPPARDELLE WITH FRESH MOREL SAUCE

BORGATTI'S RAVIOLI & EGG NOODLES /
SERVES 2 OR 3

A delicious combination of herbs, vegetables, cheese, and fresh pasta from Borgatti's, this only works with fresh morels, so make this in late spring when the mushrooms are at their peak. The fresh pasta should be cooked just enough to absorb the sauce. You should not be able to tell where the sauce ends and the pasta begins. This is a great recipe from Agata & Valentina.

1 tablespoon unsalted butter

2 tablespoons Sicilian extra-virgin olive oil

1 clove garlic, finely chopped

3 shallots, finely chopped

4 to 6 ounces fresh morel mushrooms

1 cup chicken stock

½ cup crème fraîche

½ cup fresh shelled peas, precooked but still firm

1 pound fresh pappardelle pasta

2 ounces freshly grated Parmigiano-Reggiano

2 tablespoons minced fresh flat-leaf parsley

Freshly ground black pepper to taste

1 Heat the butter and oil together in a skillet over medium heat for about 1 minute.

2 Add the garlic and shallots and cook for 3 to 4 minutes, stirring occasionally.

3 Add the mushrooms and cook 3 to 4 minutes, stirring occasionally.

4 Add the stock and cook, stirring, another 2 minutes.

5 Add the crème fraîche and let the sauce come to a gentle boil.

6 Add the peas, then reduce the heat and let the sauce simmer while you cook the pasta.

7 In a large pot of salted water, cook the pasta for 5 to 6 minutes, until just barely al dente.

8 Drain and add to the skillet with the sauce. Cook over low heat for 2 minutes, or until the pasta absorbs some of the sauce and becomes a little softer. Divide among serving bowl and sprinkle with a little cheese, then parsley. Pass the pepper around separately.

4. BIANCARDI MEATS

This is a real butcher shop, the windows hung with lamb and unskinned rabbit. The meat here is excellent, as is the service. The guys begind the counter seem to know all their customers' names, and lines can snake around the store. Biancardi has been operated by the same family since 1932. It's a great place to experience the ambience of an Italian village butcher shop. The place is known for its stuffed pork chops and house-cured pancetta.

RABBIT IN MUSTARD

BIANCARDI MEATS / SERVES 4

This recipe calls for fresh rabbit from Biancardi. Once you've broken the Bugs Bunny barrier and tried rabbit, you'll want to make it yourself, and this is a great way to start.

2 rabbits, cut into serving pieces

1 cup Dijon mustard

1 tablespoon olive oil

2 cloves garlic, chopped

1 cup white wine

1 cup vegetable broth

2 cups crème fraîche

4 tablespoons chopped fresh tarragon

1   Rub the rabbit pieces with the mustard.

2   In a large skillet over high heat, heat the oil, then add the garlic. Reduce the heat to medium and add the rabbit; cook until lightly browned, about 3 to 5 minutes per side.

3   Add the wine and broth. Cover and cook at a simmer for 30 minutes.

4   Transfer the rabbit pieces to a plate and cook the sauce until it is thickened slightly.

5   Reduce the heat and add the crème fraîche.

6   Put the rabbit back in the pan and turn the pieces quickly to coat them with the sauce. Serve immediately, garnished with the tarragon.

5. RANDAZZO'S SEAFOOD

Some of New York's best Italian chefs buy their seafood at Randazzo's, and a walk through the store conjures up delightful visions of zuppa de pesce, branzino in parchment, and linguine alla vongole. The cases overflow with octopus, calamari, clams, mussels, scallops, baccalà, Sicilian anchovies, and a great collection of whole fish. The seafood here is as fresh as you'll find, and the people are friendly and willing to help you choose the right combination for whatever it is you decide to cook. The selection at Randazzo's just may make you brave enough to try to make your own zuppa de pesce or cioppino.

CRUNCHY GRILLED SHRIMP

RANDAZZO'S SEAFOOD / SERVES 4

There's a reason the old standbys are old standbys. These traditional Italian-American shrimp from Randazzo's are incredibly easy to make, yet everyone you serve will be suitably impressed by your culinary wiles.

1 pound large fresh shrimp, shelled

¼ cup olive oil

6 cloves garlic, chopped

⅓ cup chopped fresh parsley

½ cup plain bread crumbs

1 teaspoon kosher salt

Juice of 1 lemon

1   In a medium bowl, combine the shrimp, oil, garlic, and parsley. Toss well. Marinate for at least 6 hours or overnight.

2   Preheat a charcoal fire to hot.

3   Toss the shrimp in the bread crumbs and salt to coat evenly.

4   Thread the shrimp onto skewers (soaked for a few minutes in warm water if wood) and sprinkle with additional bread crumbs.

5   Grill for 5 to 7 minutes, or until browned; be careful not to overcook. Squeeze the lemon over the shrimp and serve immediately.

BLUE
POINT
OYSTER
9.99

5

5

5

5

ARTHUR AVENUE RETAIL MARKET

It's common wisdom that brevity is the key to advertising effectiveness: "Just do it," "Think different," and "Coke is it" are a few of the successful slogans that come to mind. "For over fifty years the good taste of tradition, world-famous Arthur Avenue retail market serving Arthur Avenue and the world since 1940" does not. But the businesses of the Arthur Avenue Retail Market, 2344 Arthur Avenue, have been thriving for over half a century with this unterse motto painted on the side of their red brick building. And it should be noted that, unlike a lot of other advertising claims, this one is true. The retail market is really a collection of separate small businesses under one skylit roof. It was built by Mayor La Guardia in 1940 to house the pushcart vendors who were the lifeblood of this community. A pushcart spirit still imbues this covered market. Several years ago the owners bought the market from the city and formed a cooperative. Each of the vendors is a member of the cooperative, and its management is a miracle of capitalist collectivism. Most of the vendors sell food (there is

a cigar maker and a florist), but there is very little overlap in each store's offerings. Each store has its own specialty, and noncompetition is part of the unwritten code. The market chooses a president from among the vendors, but ex officio the spokesperson is whichever stall owner grabs you first. All are very friendly and very happy to share their version of the market's history. Our guide was Joe Liberatore, who used to sell his herbs, seeds, and tomatoes from a pushcart and now does the same from a stall at the front of the market. Joe could easily spend the day talking about the market and he is charming enough to make you want to listen.

MT. CARMEL GOURMET FOODS

This shop specializes in artisanal pasta—pappardelle, spaghetti, orecchiette, and bucatini—and in fine olive oil and balsamic vinegar. The olive oil here is from Gianfranco Becchina, an Italian maker who produces exquisite unfiltered, chemical-free oil.

PETER'S MEAT MARKET

This is organ meat central: every type of tripe (pork, beef, lamb), sweetbreads, kidneys, and veal heads, all of the finest quality. They also sell more popular parts of the animal, ready to be cooked. The veal rollatini and beef and pork braciole were excellent.

MIKE'S DELI & ARTHUR AVENUE CATERERS

A "World Famous Deli" that actually is world famous. Every inch of the ceiling and walls is covered with cheeses and dried sausage. There is so much food here that it would be hard to see the people behind the counter if they weren't larger than life. The deli is run by Mike Greco and his son David. Mike is the subject of a one-man show written by one of his sons called *Behind the Counter with Mussolini*, which might tell you a lot about Mike's management style but doesn't reflect his charm and willingness to help. Ham, sausage, prosciutto, and cheese are the specialties here, and once you've sampled them at the store you can order from their very complete Web site. The sandwiches here are also larger than life, arcane combinations of cheeses, Asiago, provolone, Parmesan, sausage, prosciutto, ham, and olives.

STRAWBERRIES WITH BALSAMIC SYRUP

ARTHUR AVENUE RETAIL MARKET /
SERVES 3 OR 4

This recipe uses aged balsamic vinegar from Mike's Deli. It's relatively easy to make, but we're sure you'll be pleasantly surprised to taste how well the combination of pepper and balsamic vinegar develops the aroma of the strawberries, which is great early in the season when strawberries don't have as much flavor.

4 pounds strawberries

1 teaspoon balsamic vinegar

1 tablespoon plus 1 teaspoon liquid honey

Pinch of freshly ground black pepper

1   Clean the strawberries under cold water, cut off the tops, and cut each one lengthwise into 4 pieces. Put the strawberries in a heatproof bowl.

2   In a small saucepan, combine 3 tablespoons water, the balsamic vinegar, and the honey.

3   Cook over low heat for 5 minutes, mixing with a wooden spoon. The mixture will turn into a syrup. Add the pepper.

4   Pour the hot mixture over the strawberries and toss to combine.

5   Cover the bowl with plastic wrap and let the strawberries macerate for 2 hours. Serve at room temperature.

lesale
tail
8340
THREE GUYS FROM BROO
THE ORIGINAL POOR PEOPLE'S FRI
4.99
LENNY BABY

13

BROOKLYN

Brooklyn was an independent city until it merged with New York in 1898. If it were still autonomous, Brooklyn would be the fourth largest city in the United States, with over 2.5 million people. Much of the character outsiders attribute to New York City—the accent, the attitude, and the sense of humor—was born in Brooklyn. A street sign in Crown Heights reads, "Vu Den?" ("What now?" in Yiddish), and in Bensonhurst there's one that says, "Fahggedaboudit."

Brooklyn's been called the City of Trees and the City of Churches; we'll go with the City of Food Stores. The diversity and quality of Brooklyn's food shops is without equal. It is also a borough of neighborhoods, each with its own distinct character and ethnic and demographic mix. Many of the neighborhoods, like Williamsburg, Red Hook, and Fort Greene, are gentrifying at such breakneck speed it's hard to keep track of the changes. Others, like Bensonhurst and Bay Ridge, seem untouched by time. In others, like Brooklyn Heights and Park Slope, the new residents have slowly changed the character of the neighborhoods, keeping the best of the old while adding new ideas to the mix.

Brooklyn is a massive borough with thousands of wonderful food stores. We've only just cracked the surface with the ones we've listed here. They are some of the best, but we're sure there are plenty of other great food stores out there in the vastness of Brooklyn just waiting to be discovered. While Brooklyn is definitely a part of greater New York City, it is the borough that has most retained its sense of independence, which is fitting for New York City's second city.

1. LITTLE CUPCAKE

The cupcake, a lunchbox staple of the 1950s and '60s, had just about disappeared when Magnolia Bakery opened on Bleecker Street in 1995 and started the cupcake craze. Magnolia was an astounding success that begat cupcake shops in at least two boroughs. First, one of Magnolia's founding partners opened Buttercup just across the street. Then, Little Cupcake opened in Bensonhurst, just across the East River. At Little Cupcake, Mark Libertini—who started out at Buttercup—has created a pink-and-pale-green fantasy of a '50s bakery. Customers watch the bakers at work while gobbling down cupcakes, pudding, cookies, and brownies, accompanied by one of thirty coffee choices. Libertini bakes about a thousand cupcakes daily, mixing them in small batches and cooling them gently to keep them fresh and soft. The chocolaty red velvet cupcake was our favorite.

2. PAPA PASQUALE'S

Bay Ridge is a nearly untouched middle-class bastion in the middle of a sea of gentrification. The population here is about 20 percent Italian American, and Papa Pasquale's is a great example of a traditional Italian grocery. Papa Pasquale's manicotti, ravioli, and stuffed shells—with five different cheese fillings—are surprisingly light and delicately flavored. The pasta alone would make the trip to Bensonhurst worthwhile, but just as interesting is how business is conducted at Pasquale's. The back kitchen is busy with the cooking, but all of Pasquale's business is carried out outdoors on the sidewalk. When we arrived, Pasquale was meeting with suppliers at the white plastic table in front of the store.

3. LIONI

There are many reigning monarchs in Bensonhurst: the King of Pizza, the King of Pasta, the King of Ravioli, and the King of Italian Ices. The Salsanto family, proprietors of Lioni, are the Kings of Mozzarella. The Salsantos started as wholesale cheese makers, shipping their wares to retailers and restaurants all over the country; they opened their own store to the public in 1996. The buffalo mozzarella here, made from the milk of the water buffalo, is rich and mellow. Lioni's epic-size hero sandwiches are named after prominent Italian Americans. Each comes with its own tag line; for example, the Vince Lombardi "Needs No Coaching."

4. THREE GUYS FROM BROOKLYN

This enormous fruit and vegetable stand, open twenty-four hours a day, 365 days a year, bills itself as the poor man's friend, but judging from the size and diversity of the crowds picking through the lettuce, Three Guys is everybody's best friend, regardless of income. The corner stand rivals the Hunts Point Market for selection and freshness, so it attracts customers from all over Brooklyn, from every corner of the borough's ethnic mix. You'll see women in saris squeezing tomatoes beside men in dreadlocks. The Caribbean, eastern Europe, North and Central Africa, the Indian subcontinent, and east Asia are all well represented among Three Guys customers. If you're overcome by a craving for pomegranates at 3 A.M. one Christmas Eve, just head to the corner of Fort Hamilton Avenue and Sixty-fifth Street in Bay Ridge, and one of the Three Guys staff will be more than happy to serve you.

MOUSSAKA
$6.50 LB

Sahadi's
WILD RICE
SA

Sahadi's
FETTOUCH SALAD
PINT $2.00
PINT $3.50

OKRA W/TOMATO
$4.00 LB

5

5

5

5

DRIED APRICOT PASTE

al wadi
chick peas

al wadi
chick peas

al wadi
chick peas

al wadi
chick peas

pois chiches bo

pois chiches bouilli

Trademark   Be Careful Of Imitation
Made in Syria -
Net Weight 17,6 oz. 500 g.r MFG BY Mohamed EL Shalati
                               Damascus - Syria Tel: 5231243

$1.75

al wadi
hommos tahina

al wadi
baba ghannouge

chick pea dip

eggplant dip

5

5. SAHADI'S

Sahadi's is an authentic Lebanese grocery that's been in business since the turn of the twentieth century; the Atlantic Avenue store opened in 1948. Open sacks of coffee, chickpeas, lentils, black beans, basmati rice, brown rice, white rice, cashews, almonds, walnuts, pecans, peanuts, and myriad spices line the store. The scent in the air changes with every step here. Sahadi's will sell any of these grains, nuts, and spices by the quarter pound or by the hundredweight. There are over a hundred varieties of cheese, including five types of feta and a few cheeses from Lebanon we've never seen before. They carry a large variety of packaged Middle Eastern jams, pickles, syrups, and sauces under the Al Wadi brand. The prepared foods are excellent: The baba ganoush and hummus are among the best we've tried. A few hours at Sahadi's is an immersion course in Middle Eastern food.

FAVA BEAN DIP

SAHADI'S / SERVES 4 TO 6

This Middle Eastern treat, made with Sahadi's bean paste, is perfect for the hottest, laziest days of summer, when an elaborate three-course meal is the last thing anyone feels like eating. Serve with crackers, pita bread, or tortilla chips.

1 (20-ounce) can Sahadi foul mudammes (fava beans)

1 small onion, diced

1 jalapeño, diced

2 tablespoons fresh lemon juice

2 tablespoons olive oil

1 teaspoon ground cumin

½ teaspoon minced garlic

1 small tomato, diced

1 tablespoon finely chopped parsley

1 Drain the fava beans and place them in a bowl or food processor. Smash them by hand or process to a paste in a food processor.

2 Add the onion, jalapeño, lemon juice, oil, cumin, and garlic, and mix together until smooth. Garnish the top with tomato and parsley.

6. ACME SMOKED FISH

Chances are, if you've eaten smoked fish anywhere in the United States over the last twenty years it was cured and smoked at Acme Smoked Fish in Greenpoint. The Brownstein family started smoking fish almost a hundred years ago; Acme has grown to become the largest family-owned commercial fish smoker in the country. Acme sells wholesale only, except on Fridays between 8:00 A.M. and 1:00 P.M., when it opens to the public and you can buy fish right out of the smoker at wholesale prices. Frozen and fresh fish from all over the world have been put through the Acme smoker. The variety of fish is enormous—wild Alaskan sockeye salmon, farm-raised Chilean salmon, mackerel, chubs from Lake Michigan, whitefish from Wisconsin, and, more recently, yellowtail tuna, bluefish, trout, and Alaskan black cod. First the fish are cured in a brine and sugar solution varying in seasoning and intensity depending on the species. After curing for about one week, the fish is delivered to the smokers—cold smoking for salmon and sturgeon, hot smoking for chubs and herring—and smoked over apple and cherry wood chips, with the smoke mixture adjusted to the desired flavor. Acme is out of the way, but worth a Friday-morning trek across the East River.

ASIAN-STYLE SMOKED TROUT AND CUCUMBER BITES

ACME SMOKED FISH /

MAKES 16 TO 18 HORS D'OEUVRES

This recipe using Acme's superb smoked trout gives the decidedly Anglo-Saxon smoked trout a whole new profile. The scallion, cilantro, ginger, and lime juice provide a light kick, and the cucumber cools it back down.

2 tablespoons fresh lime juice

2 tablespoons vegetable oil

1 teaspoon sugar

4 ounces Blue Hill Bay smoked trout fillets, finely chopped

3 tablespoons minced scallion

2 tablespoons chopped cilantro, plus whole leaves for garnish

1 teaspoon minced peeled ginger

Freshly ground black pepper

1 long seedless cucumber, cut into ½-inch slices

2 tablespoons sesame seeds

1   Whisk the lime juice, oil, and sugar together in a medium bowl.

2   Add the trout, scallion, chopped cilantro, ginger, and pepper to taste and combine well.

3   Top each cucumber slice with a rounded teaspoon of trout salad, sprinkle with sesame seeds, and garnish with a cilantro leaf.

7. BAKED

Red Hook once was a neighborhood of decrepit docks, warehouses, auto body shops, and sugar refineries. In recent years Red Hook has been touched by Brooklyn's residential renaissance, spurred by astronomical real estate prices in Manhattan. The sugar factories have been converted into spacious lofts, and new food stores are popping up all over the neighborhood. Baked was founded by two ex-admen and a designer, and the decor and the baking reflect their clever sensibilities. Coming off Van Brunt Street, the interior is a delightful surprise. Baked offers updated and retooled renditions of American bakery comfort food. Its marshmallows—both chocolate and vanilla—taste like they've just been roasted over a campfire. The large, beautiful, diner-style layer cakes actually taste as good as they look.

8. STEVE'S KEY LIME

Picture a summer evening at the end of a dock. You're watching the sun set over the water while you dig into a hefty slice of Key lime pie. Instead of flatboats trolling for bonefish, you're watching oil tankers glide by the Statue of Liberty. You're not in the Florida Keys; you're at Steve's Key Lime in Red Hook. Steve Tarpin's charming end-of-dock pie store is a tough find but worth the hunt. Tarpin makes real Key lime pie, using only authentic Key limes; they're about half the size of a regular lime with a lot more bite. The lime juice is mixed into a custard, then poured into a crisp graham crust. Enjoy a slice in Steve's waterside garden or take a pie home. The pies come in three different sizes and keep well in the freezer.

9. MANSOURA

King Farouk of Egypt was known for his insatiable appetite and demanding palate. Once upon a time, the Mansoura family were bakers for King Farouk and continually pleased him with their remarkable Middle Eastern pastries. After Farouk was deposed in 1954, the Mansouras relocated, first to Paris and then to the Sephardic Jewish community of Midwood, Brooklyn. Here they uphold family traditions and standards first established more than two hundred years ago when their family began baking in Syria. Today, a new generation of Mansouras will greet you warmly and take you on a tour of the exotic pastries piled high in glass cases. The barboura, a honey-drenched semolina cake, is enchanting with espresso. The pistachio baklava, the maamoul (pastry dough filled with dates), and the loukoum, with rosewater and pistachios, are also delightful. One of the Mansouras' secrets is their deep knowledge of ingredients—where to find the best pistachios, almonds, apricots, and honey. We're inclined to suggest that Mansoura is the best Middle Eastern bakery in New York.

10. JUNIOR'S RESTAURANT

For a lot of native New Yorkers Junior's is cheesecake and cheesecake is Junior's. Harry Rosen opened Junior's in 1950, naming it obliquely after his two sons. The restaurant was a success from the start, but the hit was the cheesecake, whipped up by master baker Eigel Peterson. Word of Junior's amazing cheesecake spread quickly, and in no time it was world famous. Junior's cheesecake is amazingly light and airy, with a dry tangy taste unlike any other of the species. Over the years the original has morphed into several flavored varieties: devil's food, cherry, pineapple, blueberry. On your next trek through central Brooklyn, do not pass up the chance to try this ethereal cheesecake.

11

13

CHORIZO 13.95 lb

BIELLESE HOT SOPRESSATA

NOSTRANO AFFUMICATO SALAME 16.95 lb

MOLINARI TOSCANO PICANTE 10.95 lb

PANCETTA

MOLINARI FINOCCHIONI 10.95 lb

MOLINARI NO SALAM 10.95

MOLINARI HOT SOPRESSATA

MOLINARI SOPRESSATA 10.95 lb

AIR DRIED GENOA SALAMI

DIRECT FROM ITALY SOPRESSATA 12.95 lb

DIRECT FROM ITALY GENOA SALAMI 12.95 lb

Red Delicious Apples $2.29 lb

13

14

11. PUMPKIN'S ORGANIC MARKET

The slow food movement started in Europe in the late 1980s as a reaction to the industrialization of food and wine production around the world. "Slow fooders" support local farming and cheese making using small-scale organic and ecology-friendly methods. The slow food movement has emigrated to this country, inspiring stores like Christina Cassano's Pumpkin's Organic Market in Park Slope. Pumpkin's carries fresh organic foods and dry goods from more than one hundred small family farms and businesses. We found farm-style milk with thick cream floating on top, artisanal cheeses, and the best of local fruits and vegetables. Pumpkin's is warm and friendly; it feels like a smaller, indoor version of New York's Greenmarkets, and it's a good place to reap the benefits of the slow food movement.

12. TWO LITTLE RED HENS

Park Slope's Two Little Red Hens is a quintessential American bakery, opened in 1982 by Marie Louise and Christina, two mothers who bring their good taste and playful artistry to every part of the business. The day we visited, the windows were painted with rabbits, birds, and butterflies. The bakers work in the back of the store to turn out muffins and scones, lemon bars and tarts. Try the apple carrot muffin and the cherry almond scone. Two Little Red Hens is famous for its holiday cakes—from cupcakes to large birthday cakes—decorated with intricate flowers.

13. BLUE APRON FOODS

Ted Marten and Alan R. Palmer opened Blue Apron, their classic charcuterie, in 2002. The cheese cave is a marvel. Marten and Palmer are both former managers at Dean & DeLuca, and they've put their expertise to work to create this beautifully designed Park Slope gourmet shop, which also stocks Sullivan Street Bakery bread and Jacques Torres chocolates.

14. BAGEL TERRACE

During the Revolutionary War, the Battle of Brooklyn was the last military engagement on the east side of the river. George Washington narrowly escaped with his wooden teeth intact. Today there's a new battle raging in Brooklyn—the Bagel Wars. The combatants can be divided into those who pledge allegiance to the Bagel Hole and those who swear by the Bagel Terrace. We've tried both, and we hereby plant our flag in the Bagel Terrace camp. The Park Slope bagelry's hand-rolled offerings, crisp on the outside, chewy inside, are among the best we've tried anywhere. If you're passionate about bagels, this is the place to test your loyalties. If you've never heard of a bagel, this would be a good place to try your first.

15. L'EPICERIE DU QUARTIER

From the vintage French posters and Barnier lollipops to the wooden bench in front, L'Épicerie du Quartier is a ringer for a traditional French grocery. In France the bench is reserved for the older men of the village, a place for arguing politics all day and flirting with the passing women. Here the bench is likely to be crowded with toddlers and their moms. The store displays, punctuated by antique kitchenware, are simple: local vegetables and fruits, breads, and canned goods all arranged in wooden crates. A small butcher's counter offers organic hanger steak and Toulon sausage. Here you can buy unhomogenized milk, with its delectable layer of cream floating at the top. Danielle and Jean-Baptiste Cailtet have created an épicerie filled with authentic French products that would be hard to find anywhere else.

16. DAMASCUS BREAD

Brooklyn Heights was once Brooklyn Village, then, during the Revolutionary War, Brooklyn Town, and its cobbled streets still retain their colonial charm. But near the eighteenth-century landmarks is Atlantic Avenue, home to the largest collection of Arab-American food stores in the United States. Hassan Halaby opened this Syrian bread bakery in 1928, and his descendants are still at it today, baking pita with passion. Ghasan Malti explains, "My pita are so good because each one is made with love and tenderness." This is the best pita we've tried anywhere. The other specialty here is baklava, Syrian style, and it is amazingly good, sweet without being cloying. And when it's time to total up your bill, Malti will tell you the exact tab before he hits a button on the cash register. He says, "First you use your brain, then you use the calculator."

17. NASSAU MEATS

Part of the Greenpoint section of Brooklyn is called New Poland. For an outsider, it might as well be a Warsaw suburb. Polish is the predominant language, and most of the stores feature signs in Polish and carry traditional Polish products. Nassau Meats is a superb Polish butcher shop. The line extends out the door and down the block as Polish women wait, not so patiently, to order cold smoked sausages. Inside, sausage hangs everywhere, dangling overhead like a carnivore's Calder sculpture. Every morning, Nassau's sausage and pierogi offerings are chalked on a large blackboard. Nassau carries ten different varieties of sausage, including perfect kielbasa. Everything is prepared and smoked in the store. The smoke rooms are closed to the public, but the smell of wood smoke wafts through the store.

18. BAKERY RZESZOWSKA

Look for the no-nonsense sign on the corner that looks like it was designed by the Polish Ministry of Bakeries. This is Bakery Rzeszowska. The windows are packed with Polish cakes, pastries, and bread. If you want to know what they are, ask in Polish, because no one here speaks English. If you don't speak Polish, listen to your eyes; if it looks good, it probably tastes good, especially the cheese bread and babka. And if you want to experience fine Polish pastry and brush up on your Polish at the same time, this is your bakery.

19. FISH TALES

Unlike Brooklyn Heights, its neighbor to the north, Cobble Hill has managed to keep its neighborhood feel totally intact. This Cobble Hill seafood store is as briny and fresh as an ocean breeze. The fish, displayed on a sleek refrigerated table, speak for themselves: Their eyes are bright and clear, and their skin color is vivid, both signs of the freshest fish. All the fish are labeled, with not only the name, but also where it was caught, its nutritional value, and how it should be prepared. Fish Tales also sells sushi-grade fish. To be eaten raw, the fish must be flash frozen for 15 hours at -15 degrees; if you're of a mind to make your own sushi, this is the place to buy the raw material.

STUFFED GRAY SOLE

FISH TALES / SERVES 2 TO 4

Freshness, freshness, freshness—the three most important things to look for when choosing the sole for this recipe. And the sole from Fish Tales more than meets this requirement. The subtle flavor of the sole combines beautifully with the stronger crabmeat.

2 tablespoons unsalted butter, plus more for the pan

¼ bell pepper, minced

¼ cup minced onion

1 cup cooked crabmeat

¼ cup bread crumbs

4 tablespoons heavy cream

Salt and freshly ground black pepper

4 to 6 gray sole fillets

Paprika

Minced fresh parsley

1   Preheat the oven to 375 degrees. Line a baking sheet with foil and grease the foil with butter.

2   Sauté the bell pepper and onion in 1 tablespoon butter over medium heat until tender. Do not brown. Remove from the heat. Mix in the crabmeat, bread crumbs, cream, and salt and pepper to taste.

3   Spoon 2 to 3 tablespoons of the crab mixture onto one of the fish fillets and roll to close, with the end underneath. Place on the baking sheet. Repeat with the remaining crab mixture and fillets. Dot with 1 tablespoon butter.

4   Bake for 10 to 15 minutes, until the fish is golden brown. Sprinkle with paprika and parsley. Serve immediately.

19

19

20. TIFERES HEYMISE BAKERY

In Manhattan we have the garment district, the fur district, the meatpacking district, and the flower district. In Brooklyn we discovered the challah district. Lee Avenue in Williamsburg houses a half dozen stores baking challah, each within a few blocks of the other. The best of these is Tiferes Bakery. There's no sign at Tiferes—the owners say they've been too busy making challah for the past twenty-five years. Tiferes bakes challah on Thursdays and Fridays for the Jewish Sabbath. The lines are long, and the challah sells out quickly, but if you get there early enough you will walk away with a precious loaf of this delicious egg and honey bread.

21. BROOKLYN ICE CREAM FACTORY

This is an ice-cream store with a gourmet pedigree and landmark status. Under the Brooklyn Bridge, housed in an abandoned 1920s lifeboat station, the Brooklyn Ice Cream Factory is a sibling of the River Café. The ice cream is remarkable, as are the fruit and fudge toppings created by the dessert chef at the River Café. Walk, ride, or drive across the bridge, get a double scoop of your favorite dipped in 70 percent cacao fudge, and watch the sun set over Manhattan.

22. SWEET MELISSA

There is a real Melissa: She oversees all the baking. Aside from a wide selection of pastries and cakes, Sweet Melissa is the New York destination for wedding cakes. Melissa is the Frank Gehry of wedding cake architecture. Her towers of cake and frosting are original and romantic and seem to stretch the boundaries of the possible.

23. JIM & ANDY'S

There's a picture of "Jim" on the wall of this unpretentious old-line fruit store in Brooklyn Heights. Jim was the original proprietor, who, with his horse and wagon, sold fruit around the neighborhood until the late 1950s. Jim still sits outside the store holding his cane and offering a smile to customers and passersby. This is a simple store with fresh seasonal fruits and vegetables displayed in their original cartons. Jim & Andy is a step into local history, a charming reminder of the horse-and-buggy days, that shouldn't be missed.

24. STAUBITZ MARKET

Staubitz Market is Brooklyn's entry into New York's best butcher shop sweepstakes; it consistently holds its own, offering meat, poultry, and game of the very highest quality, at about a third of Manhattan prices. Staubitz has not changed much since it opened in 1917: creaking wooden screen door, tin ceiling, sawdusted floor, antique light fixtures, and the original display cases (with updated refrigeration). The store windows and cashier's booth are trimmed with stained glass, and the wooden paneling gleams with the patina of time and use. Staubitz's meat is hand-cut under the supervision of the owners, John McFadden, Jr., and Sr. Along with the conventional cuts, they offer an outstanding selection of wild game and poultry, including pheasant, partridge, quail, ostrich, and wild boar.

PEPPER ROAST VENISON WITH SUN-DRIED TOMATO CREAM

STAUBITZ MARKET / SERVES 6

If you were a purist, you would create the sauce here by first making a homemade veal stock and then simmering it until reduced by half. We have made it easier by using demi-glace instead. Be sure to serve the venison roast with a big wine like Chateauneuf-du-Pape or Barolo.

4 tablespoons storebought demi-glace

1 cup sun-dried tomatoes

1 quart heavy cream

Salt and freshly ground black pepper

2 pounds boneless venison leg or saddle meat

Coarsely cracked black peppercorns

1 In a large saucepan, dissolve the demi-glace in 3 cups water, stirring, over medium heat.

2 Add the tomatoes and simmer until they are soft, about 20 minutes.

3 Strain the mixture through a sieve, pressing down so that some of the solids may pass through.

4 Return the mixture to the pan and bring to a boil. Add the cream and bring to a boil. Cook the sauce, whisking frequently, until slightly thickened.

5 Season to taste with salt and pepper. Set aside and keep warm.

6 Preheat the oven to 425 degrees.

7 Lightly coat the venison with the peppercorns and sprinkle with salt.

8 In an oven-safe saucepan, heat the remaining 2 tablespoons oil, add the venison, and cook over high heat, turning, until well browned on all sides.

9 Put the pan in the oven to finish cooking until rare. Timing will vary depending on the thickness of the meat. Press the meat with your finger; when it is fairly firm it should be done.

10 Set the venison aside to rest for 10 to 15 minutes. Slice and serve with the sauce, alongside buttered fresh fettuccine and seasonal vegetables.

25. HUNGARIAN KOSHER CATERING

Shmela Friedman, a soft-spoken father of ten, is the King of Kugel at Hungarian Kosher Catering. Kugel is Jewish potato pudding, made here from potatoes, oil, eggs, and salt. No onions, no pepper. The recipe sounds plain, but the difference between a light and delicious kugel and a leaden doorstop is in the hands of the kugel maker. Friedman's kugel is always perfect, whether you go for the sweet or savory varieties—apple, cherry, blueberry, or strawberry, or spinach, broccoli, or mushroom, all of them served in simple foil trays. The kugel here sells out as fast as it's brought out from the kitchen. Crown Heights really knows its kugel.

26. M & I FOODS

Brighton Beach, a.k.a. Little Odessa, is home to the largest and most prosperous Russian and Ukrainian population this side of the Atlantic. M & I has the institutional look of a Soviet supermarket, but the plentiful food on the shelves tells another story. M & I is the biggest food store in the area. The food selection would be greeted warmly in Moscow or Kiev. There's a huge assortment of very good smoked fish and meats. The pierogi are excellent, as is the enormous and tangy selection of pickled vegetables, ranging from watermelon to mushrooms. If it can be pickled you can be sure it's available here.

27. VINTAGE

Another Brighton Avenue grocery is Vintage. After the chaos of M & I, Vintage's well-ordered shelves offer a soothing visual respite. The sparkling-clean dried food display at the center of the store is a small miracle of organization, with separate boxes for each variety of fruit and nuts, and absolutely no spillover. There are dried apricots, cherries, apples, plums, bananas, pineapples, and pears alongside bins of cashews, almonds, peanuts, pecans, and walnuts. Sunflower seeds are in great demand. There's a continual skirmish between the store manager and customers who insist upon nibbling samples from the open bin. From what we can see he's got as much chance of stopping them as Elmer Fudd does with Bugs.

25

25

27

28. BIERKRAFT

In the late nineteenth and early twentieth centuries Brooklyn was the brewing capital of the country, turning out more beer than Milwaukee or St. Louis. One section of Williamsburg was even known as Brewer's Row, with more than forty breweries. The great breweries of New York—Trommer's, Rheingold, Piels, and Schaefer—have either disappeared or relocated. But Daphne and Richard Scholtz, the proprietors of Bierkraft in Park Slope, are dedicated to putting the beer back into Brooklyn. Bierkraft stocks over 600 brands of beer, 150 from Belgium alone, with brands from as far away as Ethiopia and as nearby as Brooklyn, with their own home brew sold in giant Bierkraft bottles. They make this "fresh" beer by running local beer through containers of hops to enhance the flavor. The hopping vat gurgles away in the store, and the result is tart and strong. Andrew Ager, the beer sommelier, says he's tasted over 99 percent of the beers offered at Bierkraft, a Falstaffian undertaking. Every week Bierkraft hosts a tasting, open to the public, matching five or six beers and cheeses. The tasting is a great opportunity to experience Bierkraft beer brilliance firsthand.

BIERKRAFT CHERRY BLONDIES

BIERKRAFT / MAKES 24 (2-INCH) SQUARES

This Bierkraft recipe is the best use of beer since the keg party. The ingredients are strange but the result is a blondie like no other you've had before.

1½ cups all-purpose flour

1 teaspoon baking powder

½ teaspoon fine sea salt

¾ cup unsalted cultured butter

2 cups muscovado light brown sugar

2 large eggs

1 teaspoon vanilla extract

6 ounces 66 percent cacao dark chocolate, either in chips or cut into chunks

6 ounces dried Michigan cherries, plumped for at least 3 days in Ramstein Blonde wheat beer and drained

1 Preheat the oven to 325 degrees.

2 Grease and flour a quarter sheet pan or a 9-by-13-inch baking dish.

3 Sift together the flour, baking powder, and salt; set aside.

4 Cut the butter into pieces and, with an electric mixer, cream it until fluffy. Gradually add the sugar and beat until fully blended with no lumps.

5 In a separate bowl, beat the eggs and vanilla together until well blended but not fluffy. Gradually add the egg mixture to the butter and blend thoroughly.

6 Add the chocolate chips and mix thoroughly with a wooden spoon. Add the cherries and gently stir them into the batter.

7 Put the batter into the prepared pan and smooth with a spatula. Bake for 25 to 30 minutes, until the blondies are a light golden but not brown.

CHAPTER 14 QUEENS

Even if you've never heard of Queens, you've probably been there. The borough of Queens is the site of New York City's major airports—JFK and La Guardia—and home to the U.S. Open tennis championship. Queens is New York's largest borough and the second most populous.

The area we now call Queens was first occupied by Native Americans, then settled by the Dutch and later by English Puritans, who named the area after Catherine of Braganza, the Portuguese wife of Charles II, the Scottish king of England. This founding potpourri only hints at the melting pot that is present-day Queens. Walking its avenues, you are likely to hear Spanish, Chinese, Korean, Italian, Greek, Russian, Tagalog, French, Creole, Yiddish, Portuguese, and probably some English. And every one of those languages is represented by more than one food store. Its neighborhoods are as diverse a patchwork of culinary tradition as you will find anywhere in the world. This is the borough with the greatest influx of new immigrants, and housing is relatively cheap compared with most of Manhattan and Brooklyn. When you change neighborhoods in Queens you change cultures. You can get from Cali to Delhi, or Seoul to Athens, in the blink of an eye. These communities tend to have large first- and second-generation populations, so the food stores have an ethnic authenticity it's hard to find anywhere else.

1. PATEL BROTHERS

In Queens it's a quick and easy trip from east Asia to the Indian subcontinent, a short drive from Flushing to Jackson Heights. Suddenly the store signs are Hindi, Bollywood music blares from storefront speakers, and incense fills the air. Visit Jackson Heights on a sunny day; you'll be dazzled by the vivid colors of the women's saris, and the elegance of the men in their high-collared white suits. Indians, Pakistanis, Sikhs, and Bangladeshi live side by side in this tightly packed community, and the food stores reflect each of these cultures. Patel Brothers and Subzi Mandi are the largest food stores in the neighborhood. Patel Brothers is known for exotic chutneys, masalas, and an extensive menu of prepared Indian dishes like mutter paneer and tikka masala. We were first attracted to Patel Brothers by the colorful display of Indian sweets at the front of the store; our favorite was the red laddo.

2. SUBZI MANDI

Subzi Mandi specializes in fruits and vegetables, some of which require explanation—which the owners are delighted to give. Take a pad and pencil; we asked for a recipe and looked up from our writing thirty minutes later. Some of our favorite new vegetables here are Chinese okra, Indian karela, unusual chiles, and long beans, a great detour from the usual broccoli and spinach.

SWEET-AND-SOUR CHICKEN CURRY

SUBZI MANDI / SERVES 4 TO 6

This version of the Delhi standby from Subzi Mandi is mild compared to the versions we've tried in India, but be warned: Even the mild version is volcanic. Remember to add the chile slowly, and taste as you go, as it's easy to add but impossible to take out.

3 tablespoons tomato paste

2 tablespoons plain yogurt

1 teaspoon chili powder

1 teaspoon salt

1 teaspoon ground cumin

½ teaspoon garam masala

2 tablespoons mango chutney

½ teaspoon sugar

3 tablespoons olive oil

2 pounds chicken parts, skinned, boned, and cut into bite-size pieces

½ cup chicken stock

1 medium onion, diced

2 scallions, chopped

1 Mix all ingredients except the scallions in a bowl and let sit for 1 hour.

2 Put in a covered pot and cook for 30 to 45 minutes over medium heat, stirring frequently, until the chicken is cooked through. Serve over jasmine or basmati rice and garnish with the scallions.

3. YAYA'S BAKERY

One of New York City's last remaining elevated trains runs through the old neighborhood of Astoria, Queens. Astoria is home to the Steinway Piano Factory, the old Silvercup Bread Factory (now a movie studio), and if you've read *The Great Gatsby* you'll remember that Daisy and Tom Buchanan passed through here on their way to East Egg. But Astoria now is mainly known as "Athens West," and Yaya's Bakery does look as though it belongs in a Greek village rather than under the screeching El. Yaya's is tiny, hot, crowded, and noisy. Three ovens, one of them wood-burning, run at high temperatures night and day. The owners and customers shout at each other in Greek, and you'll find it difficult to find room to turn around, or even move. Meanwhile, the train overhead sounds like a steel mill operating at full power. So what's the attraction? Yaya's traditional Greek pastries are very good, but what holds this bakery aloft is their bread, which is always just minutes out of the oven that sits three feet from the display case. Yaya's traditional Greek bread is worth all the tumult.

4. TITAN FOODS

In Greek mythology the leader of the Titans was Kronos, god of agriculture and the harvest. This aptly named Greek supermarket is the largest of its kind in the United States. Titan offers a wide choice of distinctive, tangy Greek yogurts and the largest selection of anchovies this side of the Mediterranean, more than twenty varieties. Visit the feta bar, bakery, and olive bar and spend some time choosing from the display of powerful and pungent Greek olive oils. For your next goat barbecue, check out their prepared mixed seasonings. Many of the excellent Greek products sold here are exclusive to Titan, the culinary giant of Astoria.

5. ARTOPOLIS

Artopolis is the exact opposite of Yaya's, appearing more as an American fantasy of a Greek bakery. The interior is shiny and orderly. The pastries are covered with tiny lace veils in their glittery glass cases. What Artopolis may lack in the way of authentic Greek decor is made up for by their first-rate baklava, kataifi, samali, and meomakarouna.

6. GREEK HOUSE FOODS

Somewhat more humbly named than Titan, this charming grocery carries a wonderful range of Greek products. As you arrive you'll see old folks on wooden chairs in front of the store, chatting the day away. Inside you'll find dried herbs hanging from the ceiling. You won't mind the lack of air-conditioning, since this is just the sort of store you would discover on a road trip through the villages of northern Greece.

AVGOLEMONO SOUP

GREEK HOUSE FOODS / SERVES 4 TO 6

The delicate balance between the starchy orzo and the acidic lemon is what provides the interest in this incredibly simple, traditional Greek soup. The people at Greek House told us that avgolemono soup is a must at any Greek wedding.

7 cups chicken stock

1 cup orzo pasta

3 large eggs

2 lemons

Salt and freshly ground black pepper to taste

1 In a large saucepan, bring the stock to a boil, then add the pasta and cook for 5 minutes.

2 In a small bowl, beat the eggs until foamy and add 1 tablespoon water and the juice of 1 of the lemons.

3 Pour 1 tablespoon of the hot broth into the bowl; repeat this 6 times.

4 Remove the saucepan from the heat and pour the mixture from the bowl over the broth; stir very well and remove from the heat. Do not reheat the soup.

5 Transfer the soup to a serving bowl and add salt and pepper to taste. Slice the remaining lemon and put the slices on top of the soup. Serve immediately.

SPECIAL NOUGATS
ΥΠΕΡΕΧΟΥΝ ΟΛΩΝ

ΧΑΛΒΑΔΟΠΗΤΕΣ ΑΜΥΓΔΑΛΟΥ · Σ. ΔΟΥΝΙΑΣ

5

Attiki
Attiki Pittas

Honey Attiki
PRODUCT OF GREECE

Μέλ
ΕΛΛΗΝΙΚ

5

6

7. ANDRE'S BAKERY

Vienna gave the world apple strudel and psychoanalysis, which leads us to ask—which is more therapeutic, forty-five minutes on the couch or a slice of warm apple strudel? After visiting Andre's, we lean toward the strudel. Andre Heimann has been making strudel, babka, and rugelach at this same Queens Boulevard location since the 1940s. We watched Andre make apple strudel and marveled at his skill and patience. The high-gluten dough starts as a three-by-two-foot square, which Andre stretches, rolls, and presses by hand until it is as large and thin as a queen-sized flat sheet. The dough rests on a special table that gently blows air underneath, causing the dough to billow gently above the tabletop. When the dough is nearly transparent—Andre says it should be thin enough to read a newspaper through—he trims it to fit a six-by-four-foot table. He then runs a long, thick line of filling about a foot from one edge of the dough and secures a long wooden pole on the outside edge. He uses the pole to roll the dough until the entire sheet is wrapped tightly around the filling. By the end, ten or twelve layers of dough have been wrapped around each strudel. The strudels emerge golden brown from the oven with an extraordinarily light and flaky crust. Andre's strudels are filled with apple, cheese, cherry, or poppy seeds; his Manhattan location also offers cabbage. Our favorites were the apple and the cheese, but all the strudel here is remarkable. If you're still considering psychoanalysis, first take a subway ride to Andre's Bakery. He might save you a fortune in analyst's bills, a savings you can then plow into strudel.

8. EMPIRE MARKET

College Point is tucked on a small spit of land jutting into Flushing Bay, not far from Shea Stadium and La Guardia Airport. This old Queens neighborhood was founded as a utopian workers' community and for many years was untouched by urban progress. Lately young professionals have replaced the mostly German, Irish, and Italian families. But the Empire Market is an authentic reminder of the College Point that used to be. Empire Market is run by a German-American family who take pride in the individual attention they give their customers. They sell groceries, all the standard cuts of meat, and a surprising variety of loose candy in glass jars. But the real specialty of Empire Market is the smoked meats, sausages, and bacon that they make in their own smokehouse. Different woods—hickory, oak, apple—are used for different flavors. A short subway ride from Grand Central Terminal will take you to College Point, giving you the chance to bring home some of Empire's excellent bacon.

5

11

LIVE CRABS
蟹 一打
$ 8.99 1 DOZ
1打
4.75 ½ DOZ
半打

TORTILLERIA MEXICANA
CORN TORTILLAS
LOS HERMANOS

9

11

9. HONG KONG SUPERMARKET

The Puritans who settled Flushing, Queens, in the seventeenth century named their village after the town in Netherlands from which they sailed. The Flushing of old New York was an area of farms and light industry. It is now home to the largest, most prosperous Asian community in New York City. Flushing is a vibrant mix of cultures—Chinese, Korean, Thai, Filipino, and Japanese. Main Street hums with Asian dialects, and all the stores are labeled in their native language, with only some translated into English. One of the best food stores in Flushing is Hong Kong Supermarket, which carries a dazzling array of Asian products. Start at the back of the store with the wall of fish tanks. The fish are sold alive, and in the pristine tanks you'll find stone fish, eel, lobster, donjon crab, turtles, toads, and frogs. Next, wander over to the meat section, where you'll find smoked and salted duck, smoked pork bellies, and Chinese-style sausage. Hong Kong sells more than ten different kinds of duck eggs, stronger and more flavorful than chicken eggs. If you cook with tofu, you can buy it here in blocks or in sheets that are just right for making "lasagna." For a new twist on hors d'oeuvres, choose from thirty varieties of stuffed buns. Hong Kong Supermarket is also the destination for unique fruits and vegetables—pea tips, nagaimob (sticky potatoes), lily roots, fresh sugar cane, taro, marindo (another starchy root), and water spinach. All this before you get to the pharmacy, where the wares get even more exotic. Maybe you've been looking for shark fins (to boost male potency) or edible swallow's nests (also to boost male potency or for endocrine imbalance). Buyer beware: The main ingredient in the swallow's nest is bird saliva. We passed up the chance to try this special elixir.

10. LA CALENITA BAKERY

Dilia Ramirez is La Caleñita—the young woman from Cali—and the charming owner of this Colombian bakery. Ramirez has a ready smile and will explain each and every one of her products to the uninitiated. She will also tell you what to eat with her splendid breads and pastries—and where and when. Her empanandas are outstanding; ask for the house sauce, which puts these savory pastries over the top. Then move on to the arepa, a traditional Colombian flatbread, great with cheese, butter, and salt. Among the breads, you'll find pan de queso (cheese), pan de bono (corn), and pan de yucca (manioc flour). La Caleñita's shelves display figs in heavy syrup, frunas (fruit-flavored candies), and bocadillo de guyaba (guava paste). In the refrigerator you'll find Colombian soft drinks. With Ramirez as your guide, La Caleñita is the place to learn about Colombian food and culture.

11. SUSANA'S MEXICAN PRODUCTS

This long and narrow store looks like a flashback to Old Mexico. The shop sells tortillas baked fresh, but if you prefer you can buy masa harina to make your own at home. Susan's chiles run from hot to thermonuclear, and the moles (sauces) come in green and brown varieties, varying in their use of chiles, cilantro, tomatillos, raisins, chocolate, and garlic. The flavors vary greatly from sauce to sauce, so sample some before you commit. Susana's is the source for all the ingredients you'll need for an authentic Mexican meal.

11

12. CASA RIVIERA

Queens is a borough of quick cultural shifts. The next jog took us to the South and Central American neighborhood of Woodside, a few minutes from Jackson Heights. Here we found Casa Riviera, which specializes in food from Peru, Colombia, Ecuador, Brazil, and Mexico. By way of example, from Peru there is a large selection of dried herbs, potatoes, pimientos, and beans. The Mexican wares include dried avocado leaves, scorching hot peppers, *chicharon fresco* (thinly sliced fried chips of pork skin), and dried banana. Casa Riviera's butcher shop offers salted beef, blood sausage, and Argentine meat. The fruits include two kinds of bananas for frying, plantanas verde and plantanas madura. In the freezer you'll find frozen fruit pulp—mango, guava, lulo (a small, slightly bitter orange), and coconut. Use them as mixers for summer cocktails and as the base for homemade sorbets. We also discovered several unusual varieties of sugar—fresh sugarcane and *dinas pineal,* a round block of brown sugar traditionally grated onto grilled pork or broken into chunks and dissolved in water for a light, refreshing drink. Among the sweets, we tried *velena nacional,* a traditional guava candy wrapped in banana leaves, and several thick bars of Colombian chocolate. Melt a chunk into milk, boil three times, and watch it thicken into a rich hot chocolate, traditionally served with a slice of cheese. Casa Riviera improves with each visit, so enjoy the noisy crowd and lively music. Brush up on your Spanish and expand your palate for the delightful tastes of the rest of the Americas.

SOPAPILLAS

CASA RIVIERA / SERVES 12

A sopapilla is a light and airy Mexican fried bread served with dollops of honey. These little pastries make a delicate and refreshing dessert, especially after a dinner seasoned with scorching chiles.

2 cups flour, plus more as needed

1½ teaspoons sugar

1½ teaspoons vegetable oil, plus more for frying

1 teaspoon salt

1 teaspoon baking powder

¼ cup milk, at room temperature

1 cup honey

1 Put the flour, sugar, 1½ teaspoons of the vegetable oil, salt, and baking powder into a large bowl. Mix with your fingertips to combine.

2 Add the milk and ½ cup lukewarm water and stir until a sticky dough forms.

3 Turn the dough out onto a lightly floured surface. Knead vigorously until soft and no longer sticky, about 1 minute.

4 Cover the dough with a damp cloth and let rest for 15 minutes.

5 Divide the dough into 3 equal balls, cover again. and let rest for 30 minutes.

6 Gently roll one of the dough balls on a lightly floured surface into an 8-inch square. Cut the square into 4 equal squares. Trim and discard any ragged edges. Repeat with the remaining dough.

7 Pour oil into a heavy medium-sized pot to a depth of 2 inches. Heat over medium heat until the temperature registers 400 degrees on a candy thermometer.

8 Place one dough square gently in oil. When the dough rises to the top, which happens very quickly, turn it over with tongs. Continue to turn the dough until it puffs up to form a pillow and becomes golden brown, about 1 minute. (If the dough remains on one side for too long it will not puff up entirely.)

9 Drain on paper towels. Repeat the process with the remaining dough. Serve immediately, drizzled with honey.

SUPERBOWL
SPECIAL

6 ft HERO

FULL TRAY
BAKED ZITI &
FULL TRAY
SAUSAGE & PEPPERS

ANTIPASTO TRAY

2 Doz. RICE BALLS

POTATO & MACARONI SALAD

$ 159.99 +TAX

BBQ
SPARE RIBS
$ 2.99 LB.

PORK
CHOPS
$ 2.59 LB.

CHOPPED MEAT
$ 3.99 LB.

CHAPTER 15

STATEN ISLAND

Staten Island claims strong historical ties to food. The Pig Wars, a livestock dispute between local Native Americans and European settlers, destroyed the island's first settlement in 1641. Staten Island was later settled successfully by freed slaves from Maryland and Virginia who moved north to transfer their expertise in oyster harvesting to the rich estuaries of New York Harbor.

New York City's relationship with its "forgotten borough" has always been tenuous.

For a short period Staten Island was part of New Jersey, and during New York's financial crisis in 1970s city legislators thought seriously about selling it back to the Garden State, and for their part many Staten Islanders, tired of paying taxes for services they didn't get, seriously considered secession. While Staten Island is New York's third-largest borough, it is the least populous. The feel here is more suburban than urban, and the population is not as diverse as in other parts of the city. It's a long way between neighborhoods and stores, so you should plan to visit by car. When it comes to food, the emphasis is heavily southern Italian.

Getting to Staten Island is possibly more fun than being there: You can take the Staten Island Ferry for a remarkable view of New York Harbor (no cars), and the fare, at fifty cents, makes the ferry the best sightseeing bargain in New York. You can also drive across the magnificent Verrazano Narrows Bridge, which spans Gravesend Bay at the bottom of the harbor. If you make the effort to get to Staten Island, you'll be glad New York held on to its youngest borough.

1. PASTOSA RAVIOLI

The Pastosa family started their cheese and ravioli business in 1894. Unlike other Italian groceries, which stock many brands, just about every product in the store carries the Pastosa name—the canned tomatoes, olive oil, mozzarella, even the employees, who sport red Pastosa golf shirts. Every shelf and tray sports a hand-lettered sign that gives plenty of detail about the product. This is part of what makes Pastosa's unique.

SPAGHETTI IN SPICY TOMATO SAUCE

PASTOSA RAVIOLI / SERVES 3 OR 4

The art in making this simple but delicious sauce is in perfect timing and exact temperatures. The oil should be very hot before the tomatoes are added. The high temperature caramelizes the tomatoes, giving them a softer, less acidic taste.

Salt and freshly ground black pepper

½ cup olive oil

2 cloves garlic, sliced lengthwise

1 (28-ounce) can San Marzano tomato puree from Pastosa

1 to 5 pickled hot peppers, preferably Goya brand

1 pound dried spaghetti

Freshly grated Parmigiano-Reggiano cheese

1   In a large pot, bring 2 quarts well-salted water to a boil.

2   In a large cast-iron pan, heat the oil. Add the garlic and cook over medium heat until golden.

3   Turn the heat up to high. When the oil is very hot, add the tomato puree and cover the pan immediately with a splatter screen.

4   Lower the heat to medium and add the hot peppers to taste; cook until the sauce is thickened, about 5 minutes.

5   Add the pasta to the pot of boiling water and cook until al dente.

6   Drain and add the pasta to the sauce. Toss to combine, then serve immediately with cheese and pepper to taste.

2. RALPH'S ICES

Since Ralph Silvestro opened this store in 1928, folks from Manhattan, Brooklyn, and New Jersey have come to Ralph's to "have an ice." There now are more than thirty Ralph's locations in the tri-state area. The Staten Island store looks like it hasn't been touched since the 1950s, and that's part of its charm. In Italy the closest thing to an "ice" is granita. Ralph's American version is denser and packs considerably more flavor and sugar in each scoop. Among the specialties are the Margarita ice, which, we were told, mixes well with tequila, and the Ralphiccino, a blend of cappuccino ice with chocolate and 1-percent milk, topped with whipped cream and cinnamon.

3. BARI PORK STORE

Three generations of the Buttaro family greeted us as we approached Bari Pork Store. The store flies more flags than Yankee Stadium, with a separate flag for each of the fruits and vegetables sold here. The Bari logo is everywhere—two pigs fighting over a length of sausage. After tasting, we agree: Bari's excellent pork is worth a tussle.

4. ROYAL CROWN BAKERY

The Royal Crown Bakery could double as a location for *The Sopranos*. White plastic chairs and tables cover the sidewalk in front of this Italian sidewalk café, Staten Island style. You'll understand why this bakery is packed as soon as you taste the rich cappuccino, its foam thick enough to suspend a large spoonful of sugar. Order a sandwich; the bread is crisp and fresh, stuffed with tomatoes, mozzarella, and grilled eggplant. The breads are some of the best that we've tasted anywhere in New York, especially the olive, the prosciutto, and the chocolate. If you want to linger, try a cannoli with your espresso.

ADDRESS INDEX

NOTE: Only main addresses are listed. Call or check online for other locations.

KING WAH BAKERY (26)

25 East Broadway
New York, NY 10002
212 513-7107

KITCHEN MARKET (144)

218 Eighth Avenue
New York, NY 10011
212 243-4433
www.kitchenmarket.com

KOSSAR'S BIALYS (94)

367 Grand Street
New York, NY 10002
877 424-2597
www.kossarbialys.com

**KUROWYCKY
MEAT PRODUCTS (32)**

124 First Avenue
New York, NY 10009
212 477-0344
www.kurowycky.com

LA BERGAMOTE (144)

169 Ninth Avenue
New York, NY 10011
212 627-9010

LA CALEÑITA BAKERY (249)

40-06 83rd Street
Elmhurst, NY 11373
718 205-8273

LADY M (164)

41 East 78th Street
New York, NY 10021
212 452-2222
www.ladymconfections.com

LEONARDI'S (163)

1385 Third Avenue
New York, NY 10021
212 744-2600

LE PAIN QUOTIDIEN (143)

38 East 19th Street
New York, NY 10003
212 673-7900
www.lepainquotidien.com

L'ÉPICERIE DU QUARTIER (224)

270 Vanderbilt Avenue
Brooklyn, NY 11205
718 636-1200

LEVAIN BAKERY (190)

167 West 74th Street
New York, NY 10023
212 874-6080
www.levainbakery.com

LIONI (212)

7803 15th Avenue
Brooklyn, NY 11228
718 232-1411
www.lionimozzarella.com

LITTLE CUPCAKE (212)

9102 Third Avenue
Brooklyn, NY 11209
718 680-4465
www.littlecupcakebakeshop.com

LITTLE PIE COMPANY (144)

407 West 14th Street
New York, NY 10014
212 414-2324
www.littlepiecompany.com

LOBEL'S MEATS (174)

1096 Madison Avenue
New York, NY 10028
212 737-1373
www.lobels.com

LOU CHENG MARKET (29)

57 East Broadway
New York, NY 10002
212 267-2133

**MADONIA BROTHERS
BAKERY (196)**

2348 Arthur Avenue
Bronx, NY 10458
718 295-5573

MAGNOLIA BAKERY (55)

401 Bleecker Street
New York, NY 10014
212 462-2572

M & I INTERNATIONAL (232)

249 Brighton Beach Avenue
Brooklyn, NY 11235
718 615-1011

MANSOURA (219)

515 Kings Highway
Brooklyn, NY 11223
718 645-7977
www.mansoura.com

MARGOT PATISSERIE (187)

2109 Broadway
New York, NY 10023
212 721-0076

MARIEBELLE NEW YORK (135)

484 Broome Street
New York, NY 10013
212 925-6999
www.mariebelle.com

MAY MAY BAKERY (14)

35 Pell Street
New York, NY 10013
212 267-0733
www.maymayfood.com

MINAMOTO KITCHOAN (104)

Swiss Building Center
608 Fifth Avenue
New York, NY 10020
212 489-3747
www.kitchoan.com

INDEX OF SHOPS BY NEIGHBORHOOD

MANHATTAN

INDEX OF SHOPS BY CATEGORY

INDEX OF RECIPES